C000302820

The Last of the Clan

The Last of the Clan

General Roderick Macneil of Barra
41st Chief of the Clan Macneil

Keith Branigan

AMBERLEY

First published 2010

Amberley Publishing Plc
Cirencester Road, Chalford,
Stroud, Gloucestershire, GL6 8PE

www.amberley-books.com

Copyright © Keith Branigan 2010

The right of Keith Branigan to be
identified as the Author of this work has
been asserted in accordance with the
Copyrights, Designs and Patents Act 1988.

ISBN 978 1 84868 431 7

All rights reserved. No part of this book
may be reprinted or reproduced or
utilised in any form or by any electronic,
mechanical or other means, now known or
hereafter invented, including photocopying
and recording, or in any information
storage or retrieval system, without the
permission in writing from the Publishers.

British Library Cataloguing in Publication
Data.

A catalogue record for this book is
available from the British Library.

Typeset in 10pt on 12pt Sabon.
Typesetting by FonthillMedia.
Printed in the UK by the MPG Books Group.

Contents

Introduction:
The Colonel & the General

I first came across the name of General Roderick Macneil in the autumn of 1987 when, with colleagues in the Department of Archaeology at the University of Sheffield, I was planning a project in the southern islands of the Outer Hebrides. Barra, and the islands south of it, had once belonged to Macneil of Barra and it remains the ancestral and spiritual home of the Clan Macneil. The General was remembered as the last of the long line of ancestral chieftains and as the man who had lost the Clan's homeland. He was, I was told, the black sheep of the Macneil family and he had lost the ancestral estate in a game of cards! In doing so he had not only thrown away the Macneils' heritage, but condemned his clansmen to the tender mercies of the new proprietor, Gordon of Cluny. When Gordon dispossessed and 'cleared' a thousand of the islanders (half the population) to Canada in 1848–51, then some of the blame inevitably rubbed off on the General.

Since our project was planned to last for five years and to investigate the human history of the islands from earliest times until the Crofting Commission of 1883, I began to read up on the eighteenth and nineteenth-century history of the islands. I soon found that the 'game of cards' was a figment of someone's imagination and that the General had been bankrupted by a combination of circumstances, some within, and some beyond, his control. His stewardship of the estate proved to be of considerable interest, and revealed a more complex character than that portrayed by the rather two-dimensional image of the 'black-sheep'. And his predicament – a highland chief with an impoverished but over-populated estate and a family of clansmen who looked to him to protect their interests – was by no means unique.

As our project extended from five years to fifteen, and as we became more involved with the physical remains of the nineteenth-century settlements, so I found myself becoming increasingly involved with documentary records as well as archaeological remains. Emigration, voluntary and enforced, was one of the key dynamics of this period in the islands and the part played in it by the ancestral chieftains had to be explored. This meant delving back into the aftermath of the Jacobite rebellion of 1745, into the French Wars of the 1750s in North America, and into the changing life-styles of the clan chieftains in the later eighteenth century. In this way I found myself exploring the life of the General's father, who was also called Roderick. Fortunately he never attained a rank higher than Colonel, so that he can be conveniently called 'the Colonel' to distinguish him from his son. Some of the General's attitudes, and not a few of his problems, can be traced back to the stewardship of his father.

Exploring the Colonel's long chieftainship – which ran from 1763 to 1822 – inevitably meant exploring the early years of the General's life before he himself became chief in 1822. It was something of a surprise to find that the General, as a young man, had taken part in several of the most pivotal events of the earlier nineteenth century. His experiences then almost certainly moulded his character and influenced his behaviour to his tenants and clansmen when he became chief. They also provided the platform from which he was able to re-launch a career and a reputation after the collapse of the estate in 1836. He disappears completely from public view between 1837 and 1842, when he re-surfaces in India. Following his activities there involved trawling through yet another documentary forest.

The General's story has to be woven together from a variety of strands of varying strength and colour. Some parts of the General's life are poorly documented; even the date of his birth is uncertain. Of the General's childhood we know little, but his youth is better documented, principally because he was involved in events of great significance. The best documented years of his life are from 1822 to 1836. Here we have letters written by him, others written about him, and during the collapse of the estate some very detailed accounts of his activities. In contrast tracking him down during his thirteen years in India proved difficult, despite his increasingly important rank.

But why should the life of General Macneil be a worthwhile subject for study? It must be admitted that the Colonel and the General were relatively obscure clan chieftains. They were chiefs of one of the smaller clans, and neither ever achieved greatness. They were small fish in a big pond. I recall the same charge being levelled against another general who figures in Scottish history and was the subject of a biography. The Roman general Julius Agricola has often loomed large in accounts of the Roman conquest of Scotland, and his prominence is due in no small part to the fact that his son-in-law Tacitus wrote a biography of him. In recent years, Romanists have played down his significance in the order of things, pointing out that Agricola's career, far from being exceptional, was typical of hundreds of others of his class. In my view, that is what makes Tacitus' biography of him so valuable. Biographies of the great and the good are ten a penny, those of lesser individuals are much scarcer. The story of the Colonel and the General is a story repeated many times over in the history of Scotland between 1745 and 1850. This is the story of the loss of ancestral estates, the story of the transformation of highland chiefs to lowland gentlemen, the story of the disintegration of the traditional relationship between chief and clansmen. The story of the General should be of interest and value to those with much wider horizons than Barra and the Clan Macneil.

I have refrained from breaking the flow of the text by frequent referencing of all the sources. However, the principal sources used are listed, chapter by chapter, in an appendix.

I

'From very remote antiquity': The Macneils of Barra

We can only appreciate and understand the lives of General Macneil and his father if we are aware of the social context, political history and cultural traditions of the Clan Macneil in the centuries which preceded them. In his *Report on the Hebrides*, written in 1771, Dr John Walker wrote that the Macneils had been in possession of Barra 'from very remote antiquity, the family being in possession of Vouchers for about 30 descents'. In fact, by 1770 the General's father, by then chief of the Clan Macneil, could lay claim to thirty-nine predecessors. The Macneils traced their ancestry back to the near-legendary fourth century Irish king, Niall of the Nine Hostages. Their possession of Barra they believed to have begun with the arrival of Neil of the Castle in 1030, who was credited with the foundation of their iconic ancestral home, Kisimul Castle – the 'castle in the sea'. This event was said to be recorded in the *Barra Register* a chronicle of the Macneils and their occupation of Barra, allegedly last seen in the 1880s in the hands of two of General Macneil's sisters. Such a document seems likely to have been passed down through the Chiefly line from generation to generation. In that case General Macneil himself must have been aware of its account of his family's ancestral history and traditions. However, it must be said that there is no mention of it, or indeed of his sisters, in his will.

The Macneils of Barra only emerge into documented history with the granting of a charter to Gilleonan Macneil by the Lord of the Isles in 1427. By now, however, they seem to have been firmly established on Barra and as one of the emerging clans of the highlands and islands. Furthermore to judge from their brief and sporadic appearances in documents of the fifteenth to seventeenth

1. Kisimul Castle, the ancestral home of the Macneils of Barra, perched on an islet in Castlebay. It was abandoned as a home long before Roderick the Gentle succeeded to the chieftainship in 1763.

centuries, they seem to have conformed to the pattern of behaviour of clan societies in general in this period. Social and economic relationships were guided by the idea of kinship on the one hand and by the pursuit of feuding and raiding on the other. Political relations were managed by a mixture of political and marriage alliances.

Kinship laid obligations on both the chief and his people, even if many of them were not strictly 'kin'. The chief was seen as the guardian rather than the proprietor of clan territory, and was expected to protect and provide for both the clan as a whole and his needy kinsmen individually. In his account of Barra *c.*1690, Martin Martin described how the Macneil took responsibility for both widows and widowers, and took old people unable to till their plots into his own household. If a kinsman lost cows, Macneil would replace them from his own herd. In return Macneil expected unswerving loyalty and, when necessary, that his kinsmen would follow him into battle. Equally, he exacted rents for the lands his kinsmen occupied, and in this period those rents were mostly paid in kind. Walter MacFarlane's account of Barra *c.*1620 says that 'half of their corn, butter, cheese and all other commodities' were taken each year. Since these supplies probably far exceeded what Macneil needed to feed his own family and household, much of the rent-in-kind was probably re-cycled through feasting. It was probably to supply his communal tables that Macneil kept a herd of seventy to eighty deer on the island of Muldonich. By providing lavish feasts for neighbours and followers the chief was able to display his wealth and dispense patronage.

In the case of the Macneils of Barra, their feasts were apparently particularly well-provided with good French and Spanish wines, some of which were acquired by purchase or exchange, but much by piracy. In two famous episodes, Rory the Tartar (thirty-fifth chief) seized first an English ship off Ireland and then a French merchantman, carrying Spanish wine, which had been foolish enough to put into Castlebay. Kisimul Castle had a galley house

2. The arms of Macneil of Barra give prominence to the galley which played an important part in the clan's fortunes in the middle ages and to the nine fetters which represent the Macneil's descent from the Irish king Niall of the nine hostages.

attached to its curtain wall, and the galley features prominently on the Macneil coat-of-arms and is seen on a late medieval grave-slab at Cille Bharra. Macneil's galleys were used not only for piracy at sea, but also for raiding elsewhere in the Western Isles and beyond. In 1589 a large force of Barramen raided Erris in County Mayo, killing 600 cattle and carrying off 500 hides. It may have been this raid which led to Macneil, and other highland chiefs, being warned by Act of Parliament in 1594 to cease their cattle-stealing.

Some raids took place as part of on-going feuds which were themselves the results of political alliances in which the Macneils became involved. In the mid-fifteenth century the chiefs allied themselves closely with the Lord of the Isles and joined raids on the Northern Isles which initially brought rewards in both booty and political capital, but then dragged the Macneils into dynastic struggles within the Lordship itself. Before the end of the century the Macneils had become embroiled in the power struggle between the Lord of the Isles and the Scottish crown, which led to their charter being revoked and the thirty-first chief, Gilleonan, being outlawed and forced to submit to the crown in 1505. His son and successor (also Gilleonan) also dabbled in rebellions against the Crown and in 1529 joined in alliance with other island clans to attack Argyll, Chief of the Campbells, which again brought down the wrath of the king. Further feuding led to Macneil and other troublesome chiefs being seized and imprisoned in 1540, their release only being achieved in 1543, following the king's death.

The new (thirty-third) Macneil of Barra (yet another Gilleonan), promptly joined with other chiefs in 1545 to proclaim allegiance to Henry VIII of England. The Scottish Crown immediately responded with a summons of treason against Macneil and the others, a summons six times repeated but never enforced. In 1579 'letters of rebellion and horning' were issued in the Crown's name against Gilleonan, an experience to be shared by General Macneil two and a half centuries later. Shortly after Gilleonan's death, an on-going feud between the Macleans and the Macdonalds of Islay flared into open warfare. The new Macneil, Rory Og (thirty-fourth chief) upheld the long-standing alliance between the Macneils and the Macleans and joined in violent attacks both on Macdonald lands and on the islands of Rhum, Canna and Eig. His eldest son (who came to be known as Rory the Tartar) followed the same policy when he succeeded as the thirty-fifth Macneil. He joined with the Macleans in a successful attack on Islay which was followed by the slaughter of any Macdonalds that could be found. Shortly after, however, Rory lost the Macneil lands in South Uist to Clanranald, and he was seized (but then pardoned) for his act of piracy against an English ship. The Crown decided to deal firmly with the unruly Macneils, and in 1605 Rory was ordered to relinquish Kisimul Castle within twenty-four hours or face siege and the fate of a traitor. When he ignored the demand, Mackenzie of Kintail was commissioned to capture and slay the Macneil. He remained at large, though his son John Og was imprisoned in Edinburgh and later died there.

By now, however, Rory faced an entirely new threat, a feud within the Macneil family itself. Family feuding was a common feature of clan society but the Macneils had previously avoided any major episodes of internal strife. Rory's marriage alliances now came home to haunt him. Neil Og and Gilleonan, the surviving sons of his first marriage to Mary Macleod of Dunvegan, decided it was time to ensure that Neil Uisteach and Gilleonan Og, sons of Rory's second marriage to Clanranald's sister Marion, would not succeed to the Chiefdom. A surviving court order describes how, in October 1612, while Rory and Gilleonan Og were sitting in Kisimul Castle 'in sober and quiet manner', Neil Og and Gilleonan, accompanied by twenty men who were armed to the teeth, seized their father and brother and incarcerated them in the castle. It was Rory who now appealed to the king for assistance, but though Clanranald was commissioned to seize the rebels, they were never taken, and around 1620 Neil Og became the thirty-sixth chief of Clan Macneil.

The Macneil's loss of South Uist was now partially compensated for by the acquisition in 1623 of the islands lying to the south of Barra, sometimes known as the Bishop's Isles. The lease had been held by Dougall, Neil Og's stepbrother, but he had failed to pay his tack duty for many years and it was now transferred to Neil Og. Duties levied on fishermen from lowland Scotland and England added significantly

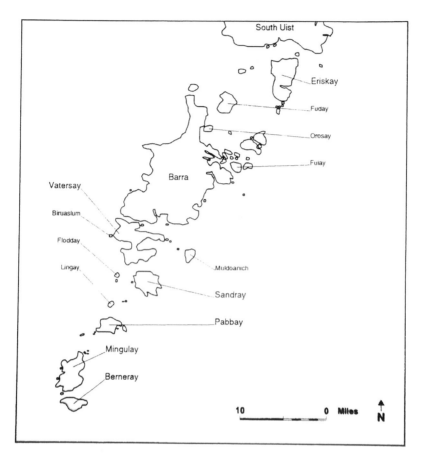

3. Barra and the 'Bishops Isles'. The Macneils acquired the islands to the south of Barra in 1623.

to Macneil's income at this time and were aggressively collected by him and other chiefs in the Long Island. A political alliance with the Macleods was maintained, and a new one developed with Mackenzie of Seaforth. A new force to be reckoned with appeared in the shape of Irish Franciscan missionaries who set out to reclaim the Western Isles for the Catholic faith at this time. The people of Barra had been Catholic from the early middle ages, but the arrival of the Catholic priest Cornelius Ward on the island in 1625 seems to have been met with great enthusiasm by two of Neil Og's sons who were duly baptized by Ward, though the Macneil himself 'refused the faith' and even accepted a commission in 1629 to apprehend priests. However the revival of the faith was not to be denied and in 1633 Father Patrick Heggarty claimed that he had baptized over 1,200 inhabitants of the Long Island, among whom was the Macneil of Barra! Neil Og was subsequently denounced in 1643 by the Protestant minister of South Uist for keeping a statue of Our Lady in his chapel. When Cromwell invaded Scotland, the Macneils answered the summons to support Charles II and paid dearly at the Battle of Worcester in September 1651. Cromwell incorporated the Western Isles into his Commonwealth and outlawed the practice of the Catholic faith.

However, it proved impossible to enforce Cromwell's laws in the Western Isles, and under Neil Og's son, Gilleonan (thirty-seventh chief), both the population and the Catholic faith recovered. With the restoration of the Stuarts, it positively blossomed and by 1671 there were allegedly 1,000 Catholics on Barra (which must have been

4. Bonnie Prince Charlie relied heavily on the chiefs of the highlands and islands for his support in the rebellion of 1745 but Macneil of Barra was a reluctant supporter of the cause.

virtually the entire population). Four years later a Catholic school was established on the island, only the second such school in the whole of Scotland. Gilleonan, who had been baptized into the Catholic church in 1654, maintained a low profile politically but ensured that his five children all made good marriage alliances with Macleods, Macdonalds and Macleans. His son and successor, Roderick the Black (thirty-eighth chief) received a charter in 1688 which confirmed his possessions, but the following year was summoned to support the deposed James II and join the Jacobite army under Dundee. Victory at Killiecrankie in July 1689 was followed by a series of defeats but Macneil remained in rebellion at least until 1692. Thereafter old loyalties were submerged rather than abandoned and Roderick the Black was again in the field to support the Jacobite cause in the Rebellion of 1715.

His son and successor as thirty-ninth chief, Roderick (known as the Dove of the West), was again called to the Jacobite colours in 1745 but his response was to some extent ambivalent and indecisive. When Prince Charles Edward Stuart arrived off the coast of Barra on 22 July 1745, Macneil's piper was taken on board as pilot. They did not however put into Castlebay but landed on Eriskay, from where a message was sent to the Macneil suggesting that he join the party there. Macneil 'happened to be away from home' however, and there has been much speculation as to whether this was a diplomatic absence. Macneil may indeed have been concerned that the Prince had arrived with only a small personal retinue and one ship, and that Macdonald of Boisdale across the Sound of Barra had refused to get involved. The Prince and his supporters sailed on, but presumably received some assurance of Macneil's loyalty since in October a Spanish ship landed 2,500 stands of arms and 4,000 Spanish dollars on Barra to be used in the Prince's cause. News of the delivery got about, and perhaps wisely orders were sent to the Prince's lieutenant on Barra, Don Macmahon, to remove arms and money and deliver them to the Prince's forces on the mainland. The letter conveying this order implies that there were indeed some doubts about Macneil's commitment to the cause: 'If the Laird of Barra does not come out with you with all his kinsmen... give my service to Macneil of

Vatersay and ask for his assistance.' But no doubt in the hope of encouraging Macneil to take up arms, a postscript says that Macneil must be told that 6,000 French troops had arrived in the south in support of the Prince.

It may be that this ploy met with some success, for in January Macneil issued a receipt to Macmahon for the sum of £10 'to bring up my men for his Royal Highness' service' and gave him a promissory note 'to be out with my men to convey Pastich of war for his Royal Highness'. By 20 January it was reported that Macneil had 120 men ready to escort arms and money to the Prince. His activities seem to have been an open secret and Macdonald of Sleat, who held the superiority of Barra, wrote to Clanranald on 25 January urging him to persuade Macneil to hand over the remaining arms in his possession to Macdonald, thus providing him with a 'pretext of keeping Barra free from any molestation'.

There is no evidence that Clanranald intervened or that Macneil grasped the opportunity to extricate himself. At the beginning of April 1746, shortly before the calamitous Battle of Culloden, the Prince's aides collected £380 from Barra. They were just in time for on 8 April Captain Ferguson arrested Macneil in a pre-emptive strike, to prevent him from joining the Royalist army. Ferguson informed the Duke of Cumberland that he had found in Macneil's possession 'three chests of arms, one and a half barrels of gunpowder, two boxes of balls and some flints, and 160 Spanish dollars'. A further 115 stands of arms which Macneil had distributed to his tenants were recovered, and it was found that £500 had been sent to his son-in-law, Macdonald of Boisdale just two days earlier. This evidence, together with the documents he had signed in January (and which fell into government hands in June), were more than enough to implicate the Macneil in the lost Jacobite cause.

After being questioned by General Campbell, Roderick was taken to Inverness, and was transported to London on the prison ship *Pamela*, which anchored off Tilbury on 27 August. Macneil and the other Jacobite prisoners were kept on board, sustained by a ration of ½lb bread and ¼lb of cheese a day. On 1 November Macneil was transferred from the prison ship to custody in a private house. He was held here throughout the winter of 1746–7, during which time some of his clansmen were interrogated about his activities. Then, somewhat abruptly, on 29 May, an order was made for the Macneil's discharge. Furthermore his estate was not confiscated but returned to him under the continuing superiority of Macdonald of Sleat. It has been claimed that Macneil turned 'king's evidence'. But Macdonald of Sleat was regarded as a 'zealous friend' of the government and it may be that it was his unrelenting and generous support of Macneil that led to the chief's lenient treatment.

In fact, Macneil of Barra's involvement in the Jacobite rebellion of 1745–6 was largely peripheral. He had certainly offered his support to the Prince and had harboured both weapons and money for the cause. Further, he had given commitments to lead men to the Prince's standard. But in the event he had never taken his men into battle, or anywhere else, on the Prince's behalf. Only two Barramen appear in the Prince's muster at Culloden, and they are John and Roger Macneil from Vatersay. They were perhaps there at the instigation of Donald Macneil of Vatersay's son, Hector, who after the collapse of the revolt was arrested, imprisoned and died in custody. Ironically, it had been Donald Macneil of Vatersay who had led the Protestant fight-back against Catholicism in Barra and the southern isles, successfully campaigning for the establishment of a Protestant school on Barra in 1729.

Despite Macneil of Barra's release and the return of his estates, the Jacobite rebellion and its collapse brought about a dramatic change in the fortunes and character of the Macneil chieftainship. Before the '45, the Macneils had largely continued to behave much as they had done for the previous four centuries or more. They had offered leadership and protection to their clansmen, while indulging in raiding, piracy and feuding to enhance both their wealth and their prestige. They had used both marriage and political alliances to the same ends, but throughout they had for the most part remained loyal to the Catholic Church. And despite increasing pressure from first the Scottish and then the English crown, they had retained a degree of independence and a firm commitment to their island home. All of this was about to change.

2

'A very genteel young man': Colonel Roderick Macneil – Gentleman Farmer

When Macneil returned from his imprisonment in London, along with Catholics throughout the highlands he faced a whole series of punitive laws which were enacted to crush support not only for the Stuart cause but also for the Catholic faith. Catholics were denied the opportunity to acquire property by either purchase or by deed of gift, and after the age of fifteen they were unable to inherit estates. They could become neither governors nor schoolmasters. Worst of all, children in the care of Catholic parents were to be removed and entrusted to a 'well-affected friend', the financial burden being met by the sale of their parents' property. Many of these prohibitions had little affect on the mass of the population who owned neither land nor much in the way of material goods, and who would not aspire to be governors or teachers. Equally, it was obviously impossible for the children of all these Catholic families to be placed in the care of the handful of Protestant 'friends'. So it is not surprising that twenty years after the rebellion, Walker found only fifty Protestants among the 1,300 people of Barra. But the punitive legislation hit the Catholic lairds much harder and every highland chief, including Macneil, apostatized in the years following the '45.

Just ten years after old Roderick was released from his imprisonment as a traitor against the Crown, his son swore allegiance to King George and was gazetted as Lieutenant Roderick Macneil in Fraser's 78th Highland regiment of foot. The young Roderick, who in Clan history came to be known as 'The Resolute', had three children by his second wife, Anne Macneil of Vatersay, including one son, inevitably christened Roderick. The old Macneil was by now living at Borve, Kisimul Castle having been abandoned and falling into ruin, and it was probably here that his grandson was born around 1755. In 1758 Roderick the Resolute with thirty-one (some say about sixty) of his clansmen alongside him, sailed with the Highlanders for Nova Scotia to join in the attack on the French stronghold of Louisburg on the western tip of Cape Breton. On 26 July, after a siege, the French garrison capitulated. The following summer Roderick and the Highlanders sailed from Louisburg as part of General Wolfe's army to attack Quebec. On the night of 12 September he and his men climbed the steep, narrow path to the Heights of Abraham outside the city, and by morning were in position ready to face General Montcalm's troops. In the ensuing battle Roderick was mortally wounded. Some accounts say he died the same day, others that with a jaw broken by a musket ball he clung to life for three weeks. In any event, the heir to the chieftainship of Clan Macneil died and was buried at Quebec, leaving the future of the Clan and its estate in the hands of a sexagenarian and a toddler.

They both survived the smallpox epidemic of 1758, which killed eighty on the island, and the 'epidemical fever' of 1762 which carried

5. The reconstructed fort at Louisbourg, Cape Breton, where the General's grandfather fought the French in 1758.

off another seventy islanders. But old Roderick Macneil himself died in 1763 at the age of seventy and his grandson found himself fortieth chief of the Clan Macneil at around the age of eight. The estate he inherited carried unspecified debts as well as annuities for three female members of the family. He was taken under the wing of his uncle, Angus Macneil of Vatersay. He was not only a Protestant, but a Presbyterian minister to boot, and the young chief was almost certainly educated from this time forth in the school on Barra supported by the Society for the Propagation of Christian Knowledge. Inevitably the young Macneil became a Protestant and in doing so erected a barrier between himself and his still overwhelmingly Catholic clansmen and tenants. Later he was sent to school in Aberdeen, because the meagre £30 per annum available to pay for the children's education was insufficient to meet the cost of schooling in Edinburgh or Glasgow. He matriculated at Glasgow University in 1769 but he does not appear in the lists of alumni of any Scottish university and penury presumably prevented him from pursuing his education to a higher level. Roderick the Gentle, as he became known, probably spent his later teens on Barra, learning how to be a Protestant, a land-owner, and a clan chieftain.

On neighbouring South Uist in 1769, Colin Macdonald of Boisdale, having converted to the Protestant faith, threatened to evict his Catholic tenants unless they too abandoned their religion. The Catholic Church was alarmed that people like the Macneil of Barra, under the influence of his uncle, might follow Macdonald's example. They immediately put up money to acquire land in Prince Edward Island and assist a large party of Catholic tenants to emigrate. The intention was not only to free them from persecution, but also to 'warn off' Boisdale and other Protestant lairds from any further attempts to convert their Catholic tenants. John Macdonald of Glenaladale, a tacksman of Clanranald, agreed to organize and lead the emigrants and set about recruiting 200 Catholics. Most were to come from South Uist, but it is clear that negotiations were also underway with the Catholic priest of Barra, Alexander Macdonald, to find some of the emigrant party from Macneil's tenants. And so, in 1772, at the age of seventeen, Roderick the Gentle had his first encounter with a phenomenon which was to return to plague him time and again during his lifetime – the 'spirit of emigration'. In the event he lost eight tenants and their families, lured away from their one or two acres held on annual leases to take plots of 150 acres held on leases which would run for 3,000 years! They were also provided with a priest to minister to their spiritual needs.

Six years later Roderick himself followed in the footsteps of the emigrants and sailed for America, but like his father before him he was seeking not a new home but military glory.

When the young Duke of Hamilton raised a regiment (the 82nd, Duke of Hamilton's) to fight the American rebels in 1778, Roderick joined up and appears to have taken a detachment of Barramen with him just as his father had done twenty years before. The Duke offered handsome bounties to new recruits and the Macneil may not have needed to resort to his chiefly rank to induce his men to join him. Macneil himself was appointed a lieutenant in the new regiment. In August 1778 they arrived in Halifax, Nova Scotia, where they initially joined the garrison, but probably spent the cold Canadian winter under canvas, the new citadel having not yet been built. In June the following year they were sent under the command of Brigadier General Maclean to build and garrison a fort on the Bay of Penobscot in Maine, intended to harass and prevent maritime trade into Boston. At the end of July an American force from Boston effected a landing near the fort but were repulsed by soldiers of the 82nd, led by a young Lieutenant, John Moore. At some point in the 82nd's service in America, John Moore and Roderick Macneil became good friends. It was a friendship maintained down the years and which was to have important consequences for Roderick's son thirty years later.

The 82nd regiment shortly after returned to Halifax before being dispatched to New York and from there, at the end of 1780, to Charleston, North Carolina. Now part of Lord Cornwallis's army they took part in the battle at Guilford Court House in March 1781 and it may have been here that Roderick the Gentle received an injury to his wrist which became infected. Thereafter the army, after a series of marches, ended up at Yorktown. The 82nd regiment were stationed across the river at Gloucester, but surrendered to the Americans along with the rest of Cornwallis's force on 19 October 1781. Roderick and his colleagues now found themselves prisoners and they were transported to New York where they remained until the war ended and they sailed back to Halifax in October 1783. At least fifteen Barramen who had fought in the war decided to settle in British North America, taking up grants of land in the area of Cape St George and Malignant Cove on the north coast of Nova Scotia. But the Macneil was not among them. He returned home and is recorded alongside some of his clansmen in a 'signing off' roll of June 1784, following the disbandment of the regiment. He was now nearly thirty years old, he had seen and experienced the New World, and had suffered the pain and deprivations of war. But his estate had been neglected while he was in America and now required his attention.

Possibly his service in the New World had widened his horizons for soon after his return he took himself off to Europe and in particular to the Low Countries where he took a close interest in new developments in raising livestock and farming in general. When he returned to Barra he at once began to completely reorganize his estate. Whereas his grandfather had lived in Borve, he created a large 'home farm' on the Eoligarry peninsula at the north end of Barra, an area predominantly of light machair soils suitable for both cattle-raising and cultivation. He bought selected cattle from a variety of mainland herds and created a herd 'of his own rearing equal to any of them' according to the Reverend Macqueen, the Church of Scotland minister on Barra. He also used plough cultivation extensively and encouraged his tenants to do likewise. A second farm was created for Macneil at Caolis on the north end of Vatersay, an area with less machair and more rough grazing suitable mainly for sheep. In addition to these two extensive farms of his own, Macneil created five farms on the west of Barra that he rented out for nineteen years at a fixed rent.

The creation of these farms inevitably impacted directly on his small tenants and clansmen. In the case of the home farm at Eoligarry the tenants were evicted and removed to new small holdings elsewhere on Barra. The west coast farms also saw small tenants lose their crofts, some probably being employed as labourers on the new farms and others again moved onto poorer lands on the east and south of the island. Other measures introduced by Roderick the Gentle also directly affected the lives of his small tenants. He built a mill at Northbay to which his tenants were forced to bring their grain for grinding, a service for which they were of course expected to pay. At the same time the productivity of their land was reduced by their being prohibited from manuring it in the traditional way with seaweed, which the laird now wanted to be collected for kelp production. So, in a variety of ways, Macneil's zeal to improve his estate and its management began to break down the traditional protective relationship of laird to clansman.

6. The surviving gable-end of Macneil's mill at Northbay, built by Roderick the Gentle. His tenants had their hand-querns confiscated and were forced to use the mill.

Equally, by removing himself from Borve to the relatively isolated Eoligarry peninsula Roderick made himself more remote from his people. The effect was compounded by his decision to invest in the construction of a fine new Adams-style mansion near Cille Bharra. It was an imposing building of two stories with a basement and an attic (which was added later). Approached up a flight of seven steps, the front door was flanked by four stone pilasters. A large entrance hall provided access on one side to a drawing room and on the other to a dining room and pantry. From the hall, an impressive staircase led to the four bedrooms and bathroom on the first floor. The basement housed a kitchen, laundry room, larder and store rooms, while a wing built onto the rear of the house provided five bedrooms and a bathroom for servants, and two more storerooms. Outbuildings included a ten-stall stable, two loose boxes, a nine-stalled byre, two sheds for calves, and a bull house. The outbuildings stood inside an acre of garden enclosed within a 3m-high wall. Barra House,

7. Barra House (later renamed Eoligarry House), the mansion built at the north end of the island by Roderick the Gentle and the boyhood home of the General.

splendid as it was, was in every way alien to the Isle of Barra, in its design, materials and style, and in the society which it housed. It was a building more at home in the cities and towns of the mainland and in complete contrast to the low, thatched-roofed, single-roomed houses in which Macneil's tenants lived. It was the home not of a highlander or a clan chief, but rather of a gentleman.

And a gentleman is how Roderick now saw himself, and how he had himself portrayed by the leading portrait painter of his day, Sir Henry Raeburn. The portrait, which is now in a private collection in the USA, shows the fortieth chief of the Clan Macneil wearing a three-quarter length green coat with a black velvet collar, buff breaches and a white jabot. He holds a hunting gun in his left arm, a large floppy hat in his right hand, and he stands, rather nonchalantly, in a hilly landscape with trees. Raeburn also painted Roderick's new wife, Jean Cameron of Fassifern, whom he had married in Edinburgh on 4 April in 1788. Unlike her husband, the Fair Lady of Barra is seated on a drape-covered bench and wears a full-length white dress with a black sash. Her father, writing to inform a friend of the wedding, described his new son-in-law as 'a very genteel young man' and that is a description of which Roderick himself almost certainly would have approved.

A growing sense of alienation between the Protestant landlord and his Catholic tenants seems to have come to a head in March 1790. Roderick had already provided funds for the Society for the Propagation of Christian Knowledge to build a school and a house for its master. In contrast he apparently refused his Catholic clansmen permission to build a new church, and coming on four of them inspecting a potential site for their new place of worship on 9 March 1790 he fell into a furious argument with them. As a result there was a threat of mass migration from the Catholics and with the encouragement of the church twenty-eight families left Barra on *The Queen* (of Greenock) in the summer of 1790, bound for Cape Breton but ending up on Prince Edward Island. A further group followed, again settling on Prince Edward Island in 1792. So Roderick the Gentle lost perhaps 300 of his tenants and clansmen in the space of just three years.

8. Roderick the Gentle, fortieth Chief of the Clan Macneil, painted by Raeburn c.1790.

9. Jean Cameron of Fassifern, Roderick the Gentle's wife and the General's mother, painted by Raeburn.

Macneil's 'arbitrary and despotic' attitude to his Catholic tenants re-surfaced in 1799 when the parish priest wrote to his bishop, complaining of Macneil's persecution and saying that 'Barra's conduct from first to last has been of a more black complexion than I at first imagined'. This episode, coupled with a widespread 'spirit of emigration' in the highlands and islands at this time, may well be behind the emigrations of 1801 and 1802. The records of these emigrations are confusing but there is little doubt that they happened and that they involved a large number of Macneil's tenants. Oral traditions suggest the figure of around 500 in 1801 and 370 people in 1802. One account, written in 1802, claims that either 600 or 1,000 people left the island for North America that year, but these figures all seem impossibly high for an island with a population in the (May) 1801 census of 1,925 persons. However, records from Nova Scotia allow us to identify by name about 100 Barra emigrants who arrived there in 1802 and there would certainly have been others that we can no longer individually identify.

Even with this significant loss of tenants, however, Roderick the Gentle was faced with the problem that there was simply not enough even marginally useful farming land to provide crofts of even two acres for all the families on the island. Some of the crofts which had been lost to farms on the west coast were perhaps now restored. The farm leases had run out around 1795, and a surviving rental list for the estate from 1811 reveals only one small farm – at Northbay – and the west coast townships reverted to small tenancies. But Macneil also resorted to the ploy of reducing the size of some of the crofts to allow him to create additional new ones. He did not, however, reduce the rent at the same time. In fact between 1764 and 1811 rents in Barra rose by more than 300 per cent. So how did Roderick the Gentle come down in clan tradition as a chief of the old sort, looking after his clansmen rather than lining his pockets at their expense? Even that scourge of the 'improving proprietor', John Lorne Campbell, believed that Roderick the Gentle was 'warmly attached to his tenants... the relationship between him and them was still personal and not commercialized'.

Some of the additional rental was paid by the tenants' income from kelping for Macneil. The collection and burning of seaweed to produce alkali-rich ashes which were used in various industrial processes was an activity which gradually increased throughout the last decade of the eighteenth century. Macneil paid the labourers on his home farm from £1 10s to £2 2s per ton, and tenants £2 12s, which was said to be 'the highest price in the Highlands'. He also allowed his tenants to make whatever they could, and chose to, of the rich fishing around Barra, which could provide both an important supplement to their diet and an additional source of income. Macqueen records that in bad years when crops were poor, Roderick bought-in supplies in bulk from the lowlands which he passed on to his tenants at the purchase price. Furthermore, says Macqueen, when some of his former tenants who had gone to Glasgow to work in the cotton mills, returned destitute to the island, Macneil provided them not only with a plot of land, but also the money to buy cattle and various farming implements. When smallpox broke out on Barra and Vatersay in September 1800, he immediately brought in a doctor and arranged for the inoculation of his tenants. It was presumably measures such as these that led John Buchanan, who visited Barra in the 1780s, to say that Roderick managed his estate 'with equal humanity and prudence' and that while 'he encourages all kinds of improvements, [he] exercises justice among his tenants and protects them from those oppressions which are too common in other parts of the Hebrides'. Macqueen and Buchanan were clearly well-disposed towards their fellow Presbyterian but even allowing for this, there is sufficient evidence to allow that Roderick the Gentle may still have harboured some of the traditional attitudes of a clan chief to his clansmen.

It may be that the raising of a large family knocked some of the hard edges off Roderick's attitude to the estate and his tenants. His first child was probably Catherine Macneil, described as his 'natural daughter' in a document of 1822, and by then married to forty-five-year-old James Macdonald of Liverpool. She is likely to have been the product of a liaison sometime in the early or mid-1780s. His first son and heir was born either in late 1790 or 1791, and was of course christened Roderick. There followed four daughters, Anne, Louisa, Catherine and Jane, a second son, Ewan and finally a sixth daughter Ewen Cameron. In 1790 the Reverend Buchanan noted that Macneil 'generally resides on his estate' and this appears to have been the case at least throughout the 1790s, so that the young Roderick and his sisters spent much, if not most, of their childhood on the island. A visitor to Barra House at this time recorded the children running around barefoot.

The situation seems to have changed with the turn of the century, however, possibly due to the rapid increase in the demand for kelp, following the outbreak of war with France. Macneil sold much of his kelp to manufacturers in Glasgow and Liverpool and he seems to have gradually spent more of his time in these places. When a new parish priest, Angus Macdonald, arrived on Barra in 1805 Macneil wrote to him from Chester. Within a few years Macneil had acquired a house in Liverpool and seems to have spent much of his time there to judge from later letters written in all four seasons of the year!

The move to England may have been accelerated both by the wish to have his children privately educated, and by the death of his wife. Mrs Macneil had perhaps found producing and looking after seven children too much. In 1796 Macneil wrote to his father-in-law to say that she had been 'strongly threatened with a miscarriage', though now better, and again in September 1800 he reported that she was ailing. She recovered sufficiently to bear further children, with the last, Ewan Cameron probably born in 1806 or 1807. By June 1808, however, she was dead, her eldest son Roderick writing at that time to his maternal grandfather that the loss of his mother he had 'perhaps not yet felt to the utmost extent'. By the end of the year Roderick the Gentle was living in Liverpool, and the younger children were in boarding school in nearby Chester. Young Roderick, however, was by then far away and in perilous circumstances.

3

'As respectable a character as any': Roderick Joins the Army

By 1808 the young Roderick was in his seventeenth year and had finished his schooling. With his father in good health and still only in his early fifties, there was no expectation that he might soon have to take on the burdens of the chieftainship and the Barra estate. He had obviously devoted some thought to his future career when he wrote to his maternal grandfather at the beginning of 1808. He rejected outright the idea that he should join the legal profession, declaring 'the law is a profession by no means inviting to me'. He was toying with the idea of a career in 'the mercantile line', perhaps inspired by his father's increasingly close links with manufacturers in Glasgow and Liverpool. But this would be very much a second choice: what he really wanted was to be a soldier. He was at pains to stress that unlike many, he did not regard it as 'a mere excuse for idleness'. Rather 'I think that an intelligent and skilful officer in the army is as respectable a character as any'.

By now, of course, the Macneils had some sort of pedigree in the army, Roderick's grandfather having fought and died at Quebec. His father had fought and suffered capture and imprisonment in America, and since then had served in the 10th Inverness Regiment of militia and had attained the rank of Colonel. Roderick's maternal uncle, John Cameron, had also joined the army and was already making a name for himself. In due course he too would make the ultimate sacrifice for king and country. Roderick's prospects of gaining a commission were therefore not unrealistic. In fact they were decidedly rosy, because his father had an important friend in high places. The young Lieutenant Moore who Roderick the Gentle had befriended during their service together in the Duke of Hamilton's regiment in

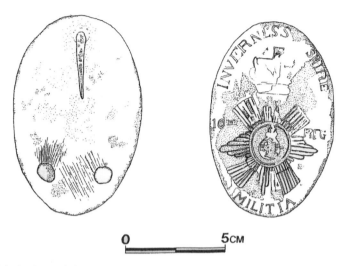

0   5CM

10. A belt plate of the 10th (Inverness-shire) Militia found at Milton, South Uist. The General's father was a Colonel of the regiment.

America was now Sir John Moore, one of Britain's most distinguished generals. Roderick the Gentle's brother-in-law John Cameron had already sought his advice and help in finding a new commission when his own regiment was threatened with being disbanded in 1802. Now, Colonel Roderick wrote to his old colleague-in-arms seeking his help in finding a commission for his son.

Moore responded immediately and on 15 March wrote a personal letter to the Commander in Chief, the Duke of York, laying before him 'the name of Mr Roderick Macneil... for one of the vacant ensignies in the 52nd Regt. He is a young man of a proper age and the son of a Highland Chieftain, an old friend of mine and formerly in a regiment with me in America'. The Duke of York was equally prompt, and just two days later on 17 March 1808 the young Roderick received a commission as ensign in the 52nd (Oxford and Bucks) Light Infantry Regiment. His father found £500 to pay off his debts and meet his expenses. In April, father and son travelled south from Liverpool to meet with General Moore, and Macneil was able to report to his father-in-law that 'General Moore received us very kindly and was so good as to take particular charge of Rory, assuring me that he would

11. Part of the letter written by Sir John Moore to the Duke of York, recommending Roderick for an ensignship in the 52nd Regiment of Foot.

be sure to see he came on'. With such an eminent patron, the new ensign's prospects for advancement were promising indeed.

Furthermore Roderick's regiment, the 52nd, was one of the elite units in the British army. Sir John Moore had been its Colonel and had trained it in light infantry tactics alongside the 95th (Rifle) Regiment at Shorncliffe in Kent. The light infantry regiments were trained to move fast, each man was encouraged to fire individually at a picked target, and to use his own initiative. In the field they responded quickly to bugle calls rather than shouted orders. Although they were still trained to fight as a regiment of the line when required, they were selected for special duties as skirmishers and scouts. A raw recruit like Ensign Roderick Macneil clearly had a lot to learn and at Shorncliffe he began a period of intensive training. He was sent to drill with a squad of newly recruited privates, learning drill movements at both a measured pace and in slow, quick and double time. He was given cross-belts and a pouch and taught the firelock exercise, and learnt how to fire ball cartridge at a target. Then he was introduced to the art of skirmishing in extended file. Finally he had to learn how to drill a company of men, and undertook a route march in full kit.

It was a steep learning curve for Roderick, and probably a hectic and tiring daily round for two months, but there were compensations. He must have cut a dashing figure in his red jacket, buff breeches and black buttoned gaiters. The jacket was embellished with a double row of buttons, embroidered shoulder wings and buff cuffs and collar. Over the jacket were whitened cross-belts with a gilt oval plate displaying the regiment's number. On his head was a tall black 'shako' adorned with a badge in the shape of a bugle, and at his side hung his sword with the same emblem embedded in its hilt. As the lowest ranking officer in the army, he was paid £160 a year. Under new regulations, he would have to serve at least three years before he might gain promotion to a lieutenancy, and another three before he could be made a major, but with such a renowned patron promotion seemed assured.

Roderick can scarcely have completed his training when orders were issued for the light infantry regiments to prepare to go to war. In a letter from Ramsgate on 3 July he relayed the news to his grandfather: 'orders have this moment arrived for us to hold ourselves in readiness for immediate embarkation'. Even while he was writing more news arrived, and he added a post script: 'our destination is supposed to be Cadiz'. This can hardly have come as a surprise. With the French driving back the Spanish forces in Iberia, Britain had hurriedly made plans to send a force to assist their allies. Initially two small divisions were to sail for Portugal, one under General Acland from Harwich and the other under General Anstruther from Ramsgate. Ensign Macneil in the 1st Battalion of the 52nd was in Anstruther's division.

Anstruther's brigade landed with great difficulty and some loss of life on an open sandy beach called Paymayo on 19 August. The scene that greeted Roderick was described by a contemporary in his memoirs: 'On one side stood the men drenched to the skin adjusting their knapsacks and accoutrements – officers mustering their companies – and regiments already put in marching order , winding slowly up the narrow defiles of the high mountains beyond on the route to Vimiero. Peasants were pouring in from the neighbouring hamlets with grapes, chestnuts, figs, wine, pumpkins etc for sale.' As soon as the men were mustered, losses noted, and equipment loaded, the 52nd moved off inland.

12. Roderick's first regiment, the 52nd Light Infantry on the march in Portugal during the Peninsular War.

Arriving at Vimiero, under the command of Sir Arthur Wellesley, they took up positions on a flat-topped hill south of the village. They had barely arrived in time for on 21 August the French prepared to attack the British positions. Alongside the 52nd Regiment were the famed 95th Rifles and Rifleman Benjamin Harris wrote a vivid description of the scene on which he and Ensign Macneil looked down at that moment: 'I thought it the most imposing sight the world could produce. Our lines glittering with bright arms, the stern features of the men, as they stood with their eyes fixed unalterably upon the enemy... The sun played on the enemy's battalions, as they came on, as if they were tipped with gold.' No doubt similar feelings of elation and pride were experienced by Roderick, but as a seventeen-year-old raw recruit of scarcely five months standing he must also have been a bag of nerves wondering just how he would behave under fire. The French attacked the British positions and Ensign Macneil found himself in the midst of his first battle. Whether he was among the three companies of the 52nd who formed part of the advanced guard and were driven back, outnumbered by the French, we do not know, but soon the whole battalion were engaged in fierce fighting. Eventually they forced the French to retire with heavy losses. After the battle, Roderick could no longer have harboured any doubts about the cost of war, for as Benjamin Harris recalled 'the dead and dying lay thickly all around'.

With the French in retreat, Wellesley was keen to pursue them but he was overruled by his two superiors, who concluded a treaty with the French, whereby the French would withdraw from Portugal but would keep all their arms and equipment and be carried home by the British Navy. When the terms of this agreement were made public the outcry in England could almost be heard in Portugal! Wellesley and Generals Dalrymple and Burrard were recalled to England. Command of the British forces in Iberia fell to Roderick Macneil's patron, Sir John Moore.

The uproar over the Convention of Cintra as the treaty came to be known, gave the British troops who had fought at Vimiero time

13. A scene from the Battle of Vimiero, 21 August 1808, where Roderick who had been in the army for only five months, had his first experience of battle.

to rest and regroup before they joined up with the rest of Moore's army of 20,000 men. Another 17,000 troops were to be landed at Corunna and march to meet Moore. Moore took the time and opportunity to reorganize his army and eventually marched north from Lisbon on 18 October, meeting up with Anstruther's Brigade at Almeida on 8 November. Back in England Roderick's father writing to Ewan Cameron on 1 November reported: 'I have no letters from Rory as they go to the interior of Spain. I doubt his opportunities of writing will be frequent.' If Roderick had been unable to write his father a letter during the month of inactivity in September then there was certainly to be no opportunity in the next three months.

As winter set in and rain made roads and trackways ever more difficult to travel, the troops suffered days of exhausting marches and nights of intense cold. As an officer, Roderick probably spent most nights as an imposed guest in private homes while the rank and file found shelter wherever they could. Two weeks marching took the army across the Spanish frontier and on to Salamanca, Moore intending to go to the assistance of his Spanish allies. But the widely separated Spanish armies were suffering a number of defeats and Napoleon himself was now in Spain with a French army of 170,000 men. On 4 December Napoleon captured Madrid. Moore ordered the various wings of his army to retreat back into Portugal and on 11 December Moore and the troops under his command left Salamanca, marching northwards with the intention of eventually uniting with Baird's force coming from Corunna. The route took the army across the bleak bare plateau. Roderick found himself marching further and faster each day in bright, clear weather which at night turned to freezing cold. When they eventually reached Mayorga a week later, Sir John Moore reorganized his army again, and Roderick's regiment found itself in a brigade commanded by Edward Paget, designated to act as the rearguard. Since Vimiero the British troops had had no further contact with the French, but with Napoleon now commanding an army of 300,000 men, closing in rapidly on Moore's 20,000 from both the north and the south, the troops covering the British retreat could be sure they would soon see plenty of action.

The main part of Moore's army retreated from Sahagun on Christmas Eve, but Roderick and the men of the 52nd's 1st battalion stayed behind with the rest of the rearguard to harass and hold off the pursuing French. Christmas Day 1808 brought neither rest nor celebrations for Ensign Roderick Macneil. Instead he had to rouse himself and his men to begin the long march to Corunna. A brief thaw had turned the icy roads into deep mud and the already exhausted troops, 'gaunt-looking, way-worn and ragged... accoutrements rent and torn and many without even shoes to their feet' made slow progress, spurred on only by the thought of the French cavalry on their tails. On Boxing Day the rearguard's light cavalry had its first brush with the French vanguard, and over the next two days there were some fierce clashes, particularly at Mayorga.

Approaching the River Esla, the rearguard halted and prepared to defend the approach to the bridge at Castro Gonzalo with a hastily erected barricade built with 'broken-down carts and tumbrils, huge trunks of trees and everything we could scrape together'. From the relative protection afforded them, the light infantry poured fire at the advancing French cavalry. Roderick's regiment, along with the 95th and 43rd, defended the bridge at Castro Gonzalo for twenty-four hours in pouring rain. Eventually, when the engineers had completed preparations for blowing the bridge, the rearguard retreated in the dark across the River Esla. The bridge was blown, with a tremendous explosion, and for the moment there was some respite for the weary soldiers of the 52nd.

On 29 December they and the rest of the rearguard entered the town of Benavente, where Roderick was able to explore the fine castle in which the retreating troops of Moore's army had been billeted. During their brief stay they had ransacked the building, as discipline began to break down. The 52nd were themselves quartered overnight in a monastery and one of Roderick's fellow ensigns described how the men found a huge vat of wine, which the prior had concealed from his unwelcome visitors, and which was now served out 'in perfect order to the drenched and shivering soldiers'. No doubt Ensign Macneil indulged himself. The next day the light cavalry again beat off attacks by cavalry of Napoleon's Imperial Guard, and in fact not only drove

14. The castle at Benavente, a contemporary picture by Robert Ker Porter. Roderick spent the night of 29 December 1808 in the monastery at Benavente, enjoying the contents of the monks' wine cellars.

them off but captured their commanding officer. It was therefore in somewhat better spirits that the 52nd and 95th regiments set off for Astorga, some twenty-five miles from Benavente.

The rearguard moved faster than the main body of the army, and it arrived in Astorga on New Year's Eve only a few hours after the last stragglers of Moore's army had left, to find that 400 wounded had been left behind. Ahead lay the steep narrow trackways that led upwards through the mountains which would afford better protection from the pursuing French but expose the exhausted troops to deep snows and devastating cold. After a few hours rest, the 52nd and the rest of the rearguard moved off again, but now they were divided into two units. One, including the 95th Rifles, took the road to Vigo, while the other, including Roderick Macneil and the 1st battalion of the 52nd, followed the main army through the highest mountains to Corunna. Roderick and his men marched through the moonless night in a silence broken only by the groans of those who had collapsed exhausted at the trackside.

When dawn broke on New Year's Day 1809, all that Ensign Macneil could see was a long shuffling line of men and horses, struggling slowly upwards around an apparently unending series of tortuous bends in the frozen trackway. Snow turned to sleet, and sleet to rain, and by the late afternoon when the 52nd reached the village of Bembibre they were soaked and frozen. One of Roderick's companions described Bembibre as 'a wretched, filthy, little hole' and to make matters worse it had already been looted of every last scrap of food and drink by the preceding troops. Dozens of these men now lay in a drunken stupor in the street – 'soldiers, women, children, runaway Spaniards and muleteers, all apparently inanimate'.

Rather than rest, Roderick and his men had to spend much of their time trying to prod the drunken troops back into consciousness and get them on the move again. Many were still there, however, when the last of the rearguard moved on again, just ahead of pursuing French dragoons who slaughtered the drunken stragglers where they lay.

Twenty miles further along the road, at Villafranca the now regular pillaging and looting had turned to riots, and Moore's army was in danger of completely disintegrating into nothing more than an unruly mob. Moore resorted to desperate measures, parading stragglers who had been grotesquely injured by French dragoons before his assembled

15. Another of Robert Ker Porter's contemporary illustrations of the retreat to Corunna, conveying the bleakness and desolation of the British retreat through the snow-covered mountains.

troops, and then publicly executing by firing squad a soldier found guilty of looting. He then returned to meet his rearguard, on whom the safety of his whole army depended, at the small village of Cacabelos.

Ensign Macneil was probably greatly heartened when his commanding officer and patron, Sir John Moore, rode into Cacabellos in the afternoon of 3 January. But his pleasure was short-lived. Although discipline remained stronger in the rearguard than elsewhere in the army, Moore launched into a tirade against 'drunken British cowards' and said that 'sooner than survive the disgrace of such infamous conduct, I hope that the first cannon-ball fired by the enemy may take me in the head'. Such a heartfelt declaration must surely have carried much weight with the son of Moore's old friend, standing in the ranks of the 52nd. But its effect was short-lived on some of the men around him who that night plundered yet more houses in the village. The next morning the rearguard's commanding officer, Edward Paget, drew up most of his force in a square and Roderick now had perhaps his first chance to see the severity of army punishment. For several hours, despite repeated warnings that the French were at hand, a succession of men convicted of looting were flogged raw. When they had been dealt with, two men convicted of more serious offences were led to a tree in the square and nooses placed about their neck. The imminent arrival of the French caused Paget to reconsider, but he demanded of his troops that if he spared the lives of these two men they would promise to reform. There was silence, and he repeated the question; still no response. But then some officers whispered to their men, urging them to make this promise, which they did, and the two condemned men were spared to cheers all round. One wonders, did young Ensign Macneil urge his company to satisfy their commander?

By this time the French were engaged with defenders of the narrow bridge over the stream below. The 52nd were ordered to quickly take up positions behind vineyard walls at the bottom of the hill by the bridge. Roderick found himself watching as the 15th Hussars and soldiers of the 28th retreated in confusion across the bridge. Close behind came the French cavalry who now charged the bridge. The 52nd opened up a deadly musket fire, and as the leading French came over the bridge and up the road they were mown down by cross-fire from the 52nd and the 95th Rifles. The French retreated, leaving the road 'absolutely choked with their dead'. For the moment Macneil and his companions could rest easy and see to their wounded. But the respite was brief for the French had crossed further upstream and soon attacked the 95th on the opposite side of the road to Macneil. As the 95th were pressed back, the 52nd were ordered to go to their assistance. A second French attack was launched to take the 52nd in the rear, but a battery of six guns of the horse artillery wrought havoc in the French lines and the attackers broke and fled back across the stream. The men of the light infantry pursued them, cheering madly, as Roderick and his fellow officers struggled to restore order to the British ranks.

The battle at Cacabelos raised the morale of the rearguard at a crucial point in the retreat to Corunna. Soon they were marching on again, in good order and high spirits, despite more snow and intense cold, to Villafranca. Here they found army commissaries destroying the supplies which Moore had wisely placed here in anticipation of a possible winter withdrawal through the mountains. They told the light infantry's officers they must prevent their men from taking either meat or biscuits from the pile they were burning. Understandably the hungry men ignored the orders and one suspects that Roderick and the other officers turned a blind eye, and indeed probably helped themselves too. Any sustenance they purloined they certainly needed, for beyond Villafranca they climbed through the highest, wildest part of the route through the Cantabrian mountains.

As they trudged wearily through the deep snow and numbing cold they passed the bodies of soldiers, women and children, mules and bullocks, who had died in their hundreds from exposure and exhaustion. Most of the men were in rags and some were shoeless. 'The road was one line of bloody foot-marks' remembered one veteran of the retreat. They wore anything they could find, and were lucky enough to come across some abandoned Spanish supply wagons full of trousers and shoes. 'The officers were also for the most part, in a miserable plight. They were pallid, way-worn, their feet were bleeding, and their faces overgrown with beards of many days growth.' Just how much of a beard seventeen-year-old Roderick Macneil could sport is uncertain, but otherwise he must have suffered the same agonies as all those around him.

Crossing the imposing bridge at Nogales, the rearguard slowly made its way to Constantino where a small but fast-flowing stream had to be crossed by a narrow bridge, overlooked by high ground. It was a good defensive position, and the rearguard was once more drawn up to halt the pursuing French. Three times the French attacked and were repulsed, but with dwindling supplies of food and ammunition Moore had to withdraw them again under cover of darkness and continue the retreat. Once more Roderick spent the hours of darkness trudging alongside his company through bitter cold and steady rain, until at last they reached Lugo. Here they reunited with the rest of the army, where Sir John Moore had drawn up his 20,000 men in a very strong position, hoping to confront the French and inflict a heavy defeat on them. But Marshal Soult, having tested the British lines and got a bloody nose, refused to commit his troops to battle.

After two days, in which the army could at least rest and replenish itself from the stores hoarded at Lugo, Moore once more ordered his army to retire under cover of darkness. Corunna was still more than forty miles away and that night the army faced some of the worst weather it had encountered. The men struggled against rain and sleet driven by a fierce wind, often losing their way in the total darkness. Roderick and his men in the rearguard had the unenviable task of having to try to round up and move on the many stragglers. 'We kicked, thumped, struck with the butt ends of our firelocks, pricked with swords and bayonets, but to little purpose' recalled Ensign Blakeney. By the end of the day 1,000 stragglers had eventually made it, and passed through the lines of the rearguard to the relative safety of the village of Betanzos. Here, there was food brought up from Corunna, and the weather became warmer and drier.

On 11 January the main part of Moore's army marched into the outskirts of Corunna. Meanwhile the rearguard once more occupied defensive positions at El Burgo, determined to hold the French at bay while the engineers demolished the bridge over the river and Moore prepared his position at Corunna. For two days, now freely supplied with both ammunition and food from Corunna, they succeeded in beating off French attacks. The bridge was finally blown on 13 January and the 52nd and its companion regiments withdrew through the lines of Moore's army to Corunna.

While they were making their way from El Burgo a massive explosion took place ahead of them, and Roderick saw two huge columns of black smoke rise into the sky and felt the earth shaking as if an earthquake had struck. In fact it was the engineers blowing up the surplus gunpowder to prevent it falling into French hands. The rest of that and the next day was spent destroying everything else that might be of use to the enemy. The rearguard having fought its way to Corunna all the way from Benevente was now resting in the rear of the army near the city of Corunna itself, with a view of the harbour below.

Late in the afternoon of 14 January twelve British warships rounded the point escorting over 100 transports, and one can imagine Ensign Macneil and the men around him cheering wildly as their saviours entered the harbour. As soon as the ships were docked

16. Ker Porter's picture across Corunna harbour, capturing the moment when the British engineers blew up the surplus gunpowder to save it falling into French hands.

the long task of embarkation began and was continued through the night. First on were the sick and wounded – and there were many of these – followed by all but nine of the field guns. Then the cavalry embarked, taking with them 1,000 of their precious horses; the remainder were shot. This phase of the embarkation was completed before daybreak on 15 January, but by now Marshal Soult's army could be seen massing across the other side of the valley.

There was no hope that all 15,000 infantry could be pulled back gradually into Corunna and embark without interference from the French. Moore knew he had to stand, meet the full weight of a French attack and repel it with such force that the French would be unable to prevent embarkation. He drew up his main force across the route from El Burgo to Corunna, centred around the village of Elvina. He placed two divisions further back on his right, where they could meet any flank attack or be brought up to support the centre and left. One of these two divisions was Edward Paget's Reserve, including the 95th Rifles and Roderick's regiment, the 52nd Light Infantry.

They took up position overlooking the hamlet of San Cristobel. Meanwhile, across the valley French troops were still arriving. Many were exhausted from the march through the mountains, and supplies of ammunition were still en route. Marshal Soult was therefore unable to complete his dispositions and preparations on 15 January.

When Roderick awoke on the morning of the 16th, he must have expected soon to be in action. But as the morning wore on there was still no attack from the French, and so shortly after noon Moore decided to begin the embarkation of his force after all. As a reward for their distinguished service in the retreat, Paget's division was ordered to march to the boats first, ready for embarkation. Roderick and his company lined up with the rest of the 52nd and began their march towards the harbour. They had covered scarcely 100 yards when the French artillery opened up. The 52nd and the 95th were immediately about-turned and marched back to where they just come from! The first French regiments moved against the British centre, but already squadrons of dragoons were moving westwards to sweep around and attack the flank of the British right. Moore ordered Paget's division to advance to meet this threat. With the 95th acting as skirmishers and Roderick's 52nd supporting them, they moved quickly through San Cristobel and then drove the French back the way they had come. Elsewhere the British centre, after buckling under the initial French attack, had held firm and a late French attack on the British right had failed to break through. By the time darkness began to fall around 6.00 p.m. the battle was over. The French had been repulsed and lost perhaps 1,500 men. The British had lost about 800. The 95th and 52nd between them had lost only 17 dead and 66 wounded. Among the latter was Roderick Macneil, badly wounded but able to embark the next day and return to England. His patron and his father's old friend, Sir John Moore, was not so lucky. Mortally wounded he died, in great pain, at about 8.00 p.m. and was buried in Corunna in the early hours of 17 January as his men made their way to the waiting transports which would carry them home.

17. Sir John Moore, Roderick's patron, was one of the most able generals in the British army but was killed at Corunna aged forty-seven.

4

'His bones are healed':
Battle Fever & Promotion

The relief at escaping both from the pursuing French and the suffering and deprivations of the march through the mountains of northern Spain in deepest winter was keenly felt by Roderick and his fellow soldiers crammed onto the transports in Corunna harbour. But his suffering was not yet over. Roderick was only one of thousands of troops who had been wounded and were now packed like sardines into the ships with little or no medical care available to them. They were surrounded by thousands more troops suffering from malnourishment, the after-effects of frost-bite and exposure, and infestation by lice. In such conditions disease was sure to fester and sure enough typhus broke out and carried off many of those who had escaped death in Spain. The conditions were made worse by the winter weather, and crossing the Bay of Biscay the convoy was battered and scattered by gales. As the ships approached England the winds again picked up and in a fierce storm off the Cornish coast two transports went down with the loss of nearly 300 men.

When the ships finally reached Portsmouth there was further delay in taking the men off. The wounded were packed into every available hospital space in and around the port, and a fellow soldier in the 52nd told his parents that 'there are about 2,000 in the hospitals about this place'. Among them was Roderick Macneil, who 'was in a dangerous state' according to his father, who journeyed south to attend him. The nature of his injuries is uncertain, but in a letter at the beginning of April 1809 his father mentions that 'his bones are healed'. In any event he seems to have spent February and much of March in hospital, when he would have had ample time to reflect on his experiences in his first nine months as a soldier.

In purely military terms they had been both eventful and successful. At Vimiero and Corunna he had gained experience of set-piece battles and known the joy of victory. In the retreat to Corunna, he had learned much about the art of fighting a strategic withdrawal. He had fought face to face with some of the cream of Napoleon's army, both infantry and cavalry. He had fought with and alongside the best light infantry regiments in the British army and under its two most charismatic and skilful commanders – Wellesley and Moore. And he had done enough to win a silver medal and clasp – even though it would only be awarded to him and other veterans of Corunna many years later. Above all, he had survived but carried the scars to demonstrate his courage. In some respects his career could not have got off to a better start, but for one thing – the death of his mentor, Sir John Moore. Had Moore lived, then Roderick might have expected to benefit from his continued patronage, but hopes of rapid advancement were probably buried with Moore at Corunna.

18. The General Service Medal and bar for Corunna, which Roderick and his fellow veterans eventually received thirty-five years after the event.

In personal terms, the Spanish adventure may not have been so beneficial to the young Macneil. Although we know little of his early years, he seems to have had quite a sheltered existence until he joined the army. The indications are that his father was a kindly man who doted on his children, who initially at least spent much of their time on the home estate on Barra where they would have led a rather pampered existence. Only the death of his mother shortly before he joined the army might have brought Rory face to face with some of the harsher realities of life, though his comments on her death in his correspondence with her father reveal no great outpouring of grief. But during his campaigning in Spain, Roderick had seen human suffering on a grand scale. He had seen the breakdown of discipline, followed by the sight of men guilty of minor misdemeanours flogged raw with 800 lashes. He had learnt to cope with the horrors of the dead and mangled corpses of fellow soldiers, and comrades suffering from hideous wounds, facing prolonged and agonizing deaths. He had seen men, women and children dying slowly from starvation and exposure, reaching the depths of human despair. And inevitably in such circumstances he had seen both the best and the worst of human nature. Men who showed supreme courage or gave all they had to help their comrades, and others who behaved like animals – stealing from the sick and dying, raping and looting the impoverished peasants they passed along the way. The horrors of the retreat to Corunna were never forgotten by those who saw them and one wonders just what effect these scenes had on the eighteen-year-old Macneil. Did they make him a better human being or give him a hard edge that he would never lose? It may be that the two months spent on the retreat to Corunna was the single most formative episode of Roderick's life.

Certainly when he was fit enough to travel, towards the end of March, there is no sign that he was anxious to rejoin his regiment at the earliest opportunity. He visited his father in his new home at Prospect Place on the then outskirts of Liverpool, and then travelled north to see his maternal grandfather, Ewan Cameron, at Fassifern where he spent a month recuperating. His father was encouraging him to seek further sick leave and, knowing Roderick's partiality for the old man, he wrote to Cameron while Roderick was with him. 'I hope he may have wit enough to take the proper steps to have his leave prolonged. Having a dash of indecision in him, I hope he may not delay taking his measures too long.' Whether or not Cameron said anything to his grandson, on 14 May, shortly after leaving Fasifern, Roderick wrote to him: 'Here I am the most unlucky fellow existing. Owing to the ride yesterday I suppose, I have got, pardon me, a very bad swelled testicle which completely prevents my riding.' Roderick goes on to say that he will be taking a gig to Stirling, and then intends to be 'laying up at Edinburgh where I shall get two sick certificates'. One certificate was presumably for his embarrassing

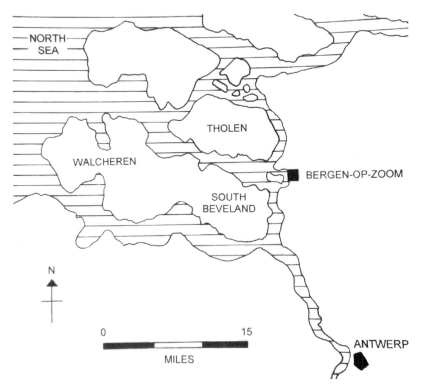

19. The Scheldt estuary where Roderick was quartered on South Beveland during the ill-fated Walcheren expedition, when 100 British troops died in action but 4,000 succumbed to fever.

affliction, the other presumably to confirm that he still needed to convalesce from his wounds.

While he was 'lying up' in Edinburgh, Roderick heard that his army (as opposed to his regimental) rank had been raised to Lieutenant. It presumably meant that his performance in Spain had been judged satisfactory, although the promotion may also have been advanced due to the number of officers who had been killed or permanently invalided during the campaign. At some point in his convalescence he also transferred from the 1st Battalion of the 52nd to the 2nd Battalion. The 1st Battalion was sent back to Iberia in June 1809 and at that time Roderick was probably still officially convalescing, which might explain his transfer to the 2nd Battalion. However, he may not have been too upset to miss such a quick return to the Peninsula.

Just when his 'sick leave' came to an end is not known, but he was certainly back in uniform and with his regiment by mid-July, when along with 40,000 more troops the 2nd Battalion of the 52nd were ordered to assemble in Kent ready to board transports which would take them to the estuary of the River Scheldt. After the near-disaster of the Iberian campaign, Roderick could look forward to this 'Walcheren' expedition with some confidence. The force was far bigger than needed for the task in hand, and it would have the close support of the all-powerful British navy throughout the campaign. The estuary of the Scheldt boasted no high mountains and narrow tracks winding through deep gorges, like the road to Corunna. With luck, the whole affair could be carried off successfully with few casualties and he could return home before the winter set in. The people of Kent turned out in force to give the troops a good send-off, 'the coast being lined with spectators to witness the splendid spectacle' as the great fleet of more than 200 warships and transports set sail.

It was a short voyage to the mouth of the Scheldt and when Roderick and the 2nd Battalion of the 52nd landed on South Beveland it was a fine summer evening and the low-lying countryside looked as pretty as a picture. After being given a supply of salt pork and biscuits, Roderick and the other officers strapped on the small black knapsacks they had purchased (at a cost of half a guinea) specially for this operation and set off to march across the island. The light infantry regiments under the command of Major General Stewart were quartered in the small, neat villages of South Beveland, whose inhabitants seemed well-disposed to the new arrivals. There was not a great deal for the troops here to do, although they could hear the guns which were pounding Flushing into capitulation. Roderick and his fellow officers occupied the first days on Beveland by hunting and fowling, and the excellent meals which their prey provided were washed down with a plentiful supply of local wines, brandy and gin. And the men in the ranks were well pleased too, with a good supply of cheap tea, coffee and sugar, and prompt payment of their wages. It was all so very different from Corunna! Flushing fell quickly, and after its capitulation, there was little in the way of hostilities to occupy the troops. Of the 40,000 troops sent on the expedition little more than 100 were killed in action.

But within a week or two of landing, troops throughout the expeditionary force were succumbing to a fierce fever. Rifleman Harris describes how within three weeks of landing on Beveland, only he and two others in his company could still stand on their legs. The rest lay weak, shivering and groaning on the floor of the barn in which they were quartered. The weakest died first, and even when the sick were transferred to ships to be carried back to England, they continued to expire.

And so it continued even after the men were taken ashore at Dover and Deal and carried into hospitals. Almost 4,000 soldiers eventually died of the deadly fever, and another 11,000 were incapacitated by it. Most of these were unable to resume their service and were invalided out of the army. As for Roderick Macneil, although we have no letters from either him or his father at this time, we may assume he escaped the fever since he continued on active service without a break from 1809 through to 1818.

As a young ensign with the experience of two eventful campaigns under his belt, Macneil was now looking for a promotion which would raise his regimental rank to Lieutenant.

With his mentor no longer able to help him up the ladder, Roderick had to find both a new commission and the means to secure it himself. Eventually in July 1810 he managed to arrange an exchange with a Lieutenant Anderson of the 91st Foot – the Argyll Highlanders. It would be nice to believe that Macneil deliberately sought out a commission in a Scottish regiment but there is little in his subsequent military career to suggest that he felt special affinity with regiments predominantly manned by his countrymen. Once again, Roderick seems to have missed a return to Spain by a whisker. The 1st Battalion of the 91st embarked for Portugal just days after he transferred into the regiment, but he took up a Lieutenancy in the 2nd Battalion, who were kept in Britain. Indeed, the 2nd Battalion of the Argylls was not a front line unit at all, but a feeder battalion, training up raw recruits who were in due course transferred to make up losses in the 1st Battalion. They were, by all accounts, a pretty scruffy and ill-disciplined lot and there was little in his new commission that seemed likely to bring Roderick opportunities for prestige, let alone glory and advancement. Nevertheless he served with the regiment, as a Lieutenant, for more than four years.

However, under a new commanding officer from 1812 they were smartened up, and the War Office decided to bring them up to strength, recruiting a mixture of old soldiers, boys and displaced Swedes and Pomeranians to make up the numbers. Eventually the 2nd Argylls were pressed into active service, joining Brigadier General Gore's brigade in July 1813 in an expedition to western Pomerania on the south side of the Baltic Sea. Landing at Stralsund they initially marched westwards through Rostock to Lubeck. Through the autumn and winter they marched on, reaching Flanders in December. It had been a long but uneventful march, and it had brought Roderick back to within a few dozen miles of South Beveland where he had witnessed the feverish horrors of the Walcheren expedition.

In February 1814 Gore's brigade were moved back to Breda where they were attached to the force which was assembled under General Graham's command to seize the French-occupied fortress of Bergen op Zoom, on the Scheldt estuary. Roderick's battalion encamped at

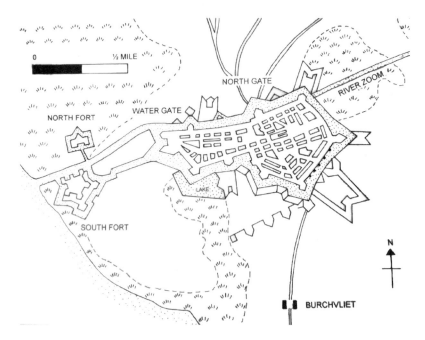

20. The highly fortified but under-garrisoned town of Bergen-op-Zoom where Roderick's battalion of the 91st Argyll Highlanders carried out a diversionary attack on the North Gate but were repulsed with heavy losses.

Halsteren to the north of Bergen-op-Zoom. On the night of 8 March the British assailed the fortress in four columns, the 400 men of Roderick's battalion forming the greater part of the third division led by Lieutenant Colonel Henry. Their task was to make a diversionary attack on the Steenbergen (or North) Gate. They opened fire shortly after 9.00 p.m. and initially took the French guards by surprise. But they were repulsed with heavy losses when they attacked the drawbridge. The rest of the British attack also faltered and fell back, suffering severe casualties and seeing many men made prisoner.

Of the 4,000 troops taking part 300 were killed, about 1,000 wounded and 1,700 taken prisoner. Roderick's battalion suffered particularly heavy losses, and Brigadier General Gore was himself killed in the attack. Roderick seems to have survived unscathed, in which case he was lucky, since thirteen of his fellow officers in the 91st were wounded.

The decision to withdraw the expeditionary force from the Netherlands had already been made before the unsuccessful attack on Bergen op Zoom, and various regiments and battalions were detached and sent elsewhere – many to join Wellington in the Peninsula. Roderick and the 240 surviving soldiers of the 91st eventually sailed back to Scotland in September 1814 and took up garrison duties at Ayr. The three months that Roderick spent at Ayr were probably the longest time he had spent in Scotland since 1808. While he and his men licked their wounds in western Scotland, the 1st Battalion of the Argylls was fighting a series of battles in the Iberian Peninsula and winning honours and medals – alongside Roderick's previous regiment, the 52nd Foot. Roderick may have felt he had made a poor career move in exchanging into the 2nd Battalion of the 91st Argylls, but an opportunity to retrieve the situation may have arisen at the end of 1814. It was decided to transfer 240 men of the 2nd Battalion to replace losses in the 1st Battalion, serving with such distinction in Spain. Whether there were vacancies for a Lieutenant in the 1st Battalion we do not know, but Roderick did not return to them. But neither did he stay with the remainder of the 2nd battalion, who were now under orders to embark for America.

On 1 December 1814, Roderick obtained a new commission, promoting him to the regimental rank of Captain, in the 60th Foot. He purchased the commission from Captain Charles Kentzinger, who was retiring. His father found the £2,000 or so that was needed to secure the post. The 60th Foot, the Royal American Regiment, had initially been raised in America in 1755 but there had been so few American recruits that it had been forced to make up its numbers by taking on Irishmen who had been rejected by other regiments of the British Army. From this inauspicious beginning the Royal Americans had gradually been built into a reliable fighting force. By the time that Roderick joined them they had a good reputation, and were one of the largest regiments in the army with eight battalions. But these eight battalions were spread, if not around the globe, at least on three continents. The 1st Battalion was stationed at the Cape of Good Hope, and the 8th in Iberia. The 5th had returned from

France to Ireland, and four of the remaining battalions were in the West Indies. The recently raised 7th Battalion had arrived at Halifax, Nova Scotia, in April 1814. These dispositions make it unlikely that Roderick had left the 91st Argylls to avoid service in either Iberia or America, since the chances were that he would end up in one or the other serving with the 60th Royal Americans. Which battalion he was appointed to is not known, and in fact we know nothing of his service with the 60th Foot. This is principally because his service in the regiment lasted just forty days.

There can be little doubt that the commission he took in the 60th Royal Americans was a career-move pure and simple, and that he had little intention of staying with the regiment, wherever it was that his particular battalion was posted. Having obtained the rank of Captain, he could begin looking for an exchange into a better regiment. Regimental agents found it for him in January 1815, and they arranged his exchange with a Captain Knipe. But this time, Macneil did more than exchange regiments, he also changed the very nature of his military service, by becoming Captain of No. 3 troop of the 23rd Light Dragoons. His three previous regiments had all been infantry units, and his translation to command a troop of light cavalry may seem a leap of faith on the part of both Roderick and the Colonel of the Light Dragoons who had to approve his appointment. We know that Roderick had been riding since at least the age of seventeen so that he may have become an adequate if not accomplished horseman by the time he joined the Dragoons at the age of twenty-three. He had also had ample opportunity to observe the light cavalry in their classic roles as skirmishers and rearguard during the retreat to Corunna. Nevertheless it was a bold move on his part to take command of a troop of cavalry.

The incentives may have been a mixture of hard cash, prestige and prospects. As a Captain in the 60th Foot he would have been paid 10s 6d per day; as a cavalry Captain he received 14s 7d a day – an instant pay increase of 40 per cent! Cavalrymen were also generally regarded by the public as rather heroic, dashing figures, an image which the cavalrymen's full dress uniform did nothing to diminish.

21. An officer in the Light Dragoons. The improved rates of pay, the smart uniform, and the public adulation of these dashing horsemen, may all have encouraged Roderick to seek his Captaincy in such a regiment.

The 23rd Light Dragoons wore a dark blue jacket with crimson facings and white lace, white breeches with hussar boots, and a black shako with red on white plume on their head. At their side was a curved sabre, which on campaign was supplemented by pistols. Roderick must have cut a handsome figure in his new uniform. And joining a cavalry regiment obviously opened up more options for him in the future, broadening his experience on the battlefield and also paving the way for a possible transfer into one or other of the most prestigious cavalry regiments in the British army. All in all Roderick Macneil must have looked forward to the coming year, 1815, with some expectation and a certain amount of satisfaction.

5

'There is a prospect of more': A Battle, a Wedding & a Death

Since the fall of Napoleon in April 1814, the British army had been reduced by 47,000 men, with many veterans, both officers and men, discharged. All Dragoon regiments, including Roderick's 23rd, had been reduced to little more than 300 men. With Napoleon tucked away in his 'gilded cage' on the island of Elba, Europe, the army, and Roderick could look forward to a period of peaceful consolidation. Roderick actually transferred into the 23rd Light Dragoons on 19 January 1815. He had scarcely had time to meet, let alone get to know, his fellow officers and men when, five weeks later, Napoleon escaped from Elba and shortly afterwards landed on the south coast of France. He was accompanied only by a handful of the ever loyal Old Guard, and initially he appeared to pose little threat to the restored Bourbon monarchy, let alone the rest of Europe. But within three weeks Louis XVIII had fled into exile again, Napoleon was in Paris, and he had begun to mobilize a rapidly swelling army. Wellington was appointed Commander-in-Chief of British forces on 28 March and arrived in Brussels on 4 April. Within two weeks the British forces on the continent had trebled from 8,000 men to nearly 26,000. As more troops arrived, they were deployed to defend Belgium and establish a common front with the Prussians.

Roderick and the 23rd Light Dragoons had been absorbed into the 3rd Light Cavalry Brigade and they were posted to patrol the frontier between Tournai and Mons. For six weeks, while Napoleon was raising, training and equipping a new French army, the Dragoons continued their patrols and saw no action. On 10 June, the 23rd joined five other cavalry regiments in an inspection and review by Lord Uxbridge. After inspecting the cavalrymen and watching them perform various manoeuvres Uxbridge expressed his satisfaction. When a French army of about 130,000 men appeared on the south bank of the River Sembre four days later, the British, including Wellington, were taken by surprise. On 15 June, Roderick's regiment and the rest of the Brigade were ordered to move to Vilvorde, and to bivouac on the high road near the town. While Roderick tried to grab some sleep at Vilvorde, the Lieutenant Colonel of his regiment (the Earl of Pontarlington) and Roderick's uncle, John Cameron, now a Lieutenant Colonel of the 92nd, were enjoying the splendours of the Duchess of Richmond's Ball in Brussels. Shortly before midnight the Ball was interrupted by the arrival of a courier with the news that the Prussians had been defeated and the French were marching on Brussels. The Ball was brought to an abrupt end, the officers returned to their regiments, and urgent messages were dispatched to all units of the army.

One of them arrived at Vilborde at 2.00 a.m. on the morning of 16 June, and Roderick and his dragoons were rudely woken and told to move with all possible speed to Quatre Bras. As they passed through Nivelle 'every house was filled with ladies and well-dressed females, who crowded to the windows, waved their handkerchiefs and cheered'. This display no doubt raised Roderick's spirits, but the march eastwards was hard work. The Dragoons floundered through the mud to Enghien, and then on towards Braine-le-Comte. It was slow going, on muddy and confusing cross-country roads and trackways. Roderick and his men eventually passed through Gemappe at about 11.00 p.m. and moved on to Quatre Bras. By the time they got there, Roderick and the dragoons must have been almost asleep in their saddles.

There was little time to rest, however. The French were coming up and Wellington had decided to retreat to take up a defensive position across the road to Brussels at Waterloo. To cover this retreat he deployed three Light Brigades and two Heavy Brigades of cavalry as a defensive screen. From this impressive rearguard two regiments were pulled out and designated to act as the final barrier between the British cavalry and the advancing French. One of them was the

23rd Light Dragoons, so as at Corunna, Roderick Macneil found himself as part of a small force given the unenviable task of keeping the French army at bay.

Roderick and the dragoons and hussars around him were perhaps able to snatch a few hours sleep on the morning of 17 June troubled only by a light shower. But as the morning wore on thunderclouds began to form and then, around 2.00 p.m., the French cavalry appeared. They swept the British rearguard out of Quatre Bras, but were prevented from following up their advantage by a tremendous thunderstorm accompanied by a deluge which drenched men and horses and turned the ground into a quagmire.

The British fell back through Gemappe, shielded by the 7th Hussars and 23rd Light Dragoons. Once the retreating army had cleared Gemappe, Lord Uxbridge ordered the 7th Hussars to charge the pursuing French lancers, which they did with some success several times until their casualties became too severe. At this point Uxbridge withdrew them and ordered the 23rd Light Dragoons to advance in their place. Uxbridge later recalled that the order was not 'received with all the enthusiasm that I expected'. Whether Captain Macneil shared this sentiment we do not know, but his regiment suffered the indignity of being ordered to give way to let the Life Guards do the job. After the Life Guards had roughed-up the lancers, the rearguard made its way back towards Brussels. An early dusk helped them escape the further attentions of the pursuing French, and Roderick and his fellow dragoons were finally able to dismount and seek a place to grab a few hours sleep in a barley field, surrounded by the rest of Wellington's army. It is unlikely that Roderick yet knew that his distinguished uncle, Lieutenant Colonel Cameron of the 92nd Gordon Highlanders had been killed at Quatre Bras.

Through the night of 17 June and the early hours of the 18th the rain fell in torrents, and neither the French nor the British can have got much sleep. Twenty-four hours of heavy rain had delayed some of the French regiments in reaching the battlefield, and slowed the flow of intelligence to Napoleon concerning the position and movement of the Prussians to the east. As a result both armies

22. Lieutenant Colonel John Cameron, Roderick's maternal uncle, who left the Duchess of Richmond's Ball to meet his death the next day at Quatre Bras.

took considerable time to deploy and in mid-morning General Van Dornberg's Light Cavalry Brigade, including Roderick and the 23rd Light Dragoons, took up position behind Sir Colin Halkett's infantry in the allied centre-right. Below them Roderick could see the Chateau Hougoumont, garrisoned by the light companies of the 1st and 3rd Foot Guards.

It was here, just before noon, that Napoleon chose to open his attack, and Macneil and the dragoons around him were able to watch the fierce battle that developed as more and more French were thrown against the desperate but determined defence mounted by the Guards. At about 12.30 p.m. 400 French guns opened up a fierce bombardment of the allied centre and left. Macneil and the Light Brigade were again onlookers as the ninety-minute bombardment took a heavy toll before the French infantry advanced, threatening to break the British line. Then the British cavalry swept forward, and Roderick could see the French infantry waver, break, and run. The cavalry pursued them but were met, and in turn broken, by a

23. The British defence of Hougmont, which Roderick watched from the slopes above, during the Battle of Waterloo on 18 June 1815.

French cavalry charge. When French cavalry threatened the guns of the Royal Horse Artillery, the Light Dragoons counter-charged and repulsed the enemy, driving them back onto their own guns. With Lieutenant Colonel Cutcliffe wounded, command of Roderick's regiment fell to Major Lautour, who re-formed it and around 3.30 p.m. led it in support of the 33rd Foot who had formed square to receive French cavalry. As the French cavalry suffered heavy losses trying to break the squares, Uxbridge led the dragoons and other cavalry in pursuit of the French.

At 5.00 p.m. the 23rd were re-formed on an eminence overlooking the battlefield and Roderick could see the thousands of dead and wounded lying on the slopes below. In the distance the Prussians could be seen advancing on the French flank. Major Lautour now led a squadron of the 23rd, including Roderick's troop, to support the British centre and drive off French cavalry attacking allied German units. Napoleon's last gamble was an advance by the Imperial Guard, which was halted in its tracks by fierce musket fire from the British guards, and then broken and decimated by enfilading fire from Roderick's old regiment the 52nd Light Infantry. When Wellington ordered a general advance Roderick's dragoons followed Major General Vandeleur's brigade down the slope, through the carnage, until the defeated French had fled the field.

The battlefield after the French had fled was a scene of ruin and desolation. Dead and wounded men and animals lay everywhere and even the victors were too exhausted to celebrate much. Regiments had been decimated and scattered, and soldiers wandered aimlessly hoping to find others of their regiment and somewhere to sleep for the night. Twenty years later, Lieutenant Banner recalled that after the battle he and some of his troopers from the 23rd Dragoons 'bivouacked for the night, when Captain Macneil and Lieutenant Dodwell with a few men, reunited with my division'.

Although the 23rd Light Dragoons had not played a leading role in the battle of Waterloo, they had done enough to restore some pride after their reluctance to charge the French at Gemappe. Major

24. The simple but elegant Waterloo Medal which was awarded to all veterans of the Waterloo campaign.

Lautour, recalling the behaviour of the dragoons under his command at Waterloo said 'they displayed in a high degree the cool steadiness and determined bravery of British soldiers'. Roderick and his comrades were each awarded the handsome silver Waterloo medal.

With Napoleon defeated and shipped off to the remote island of St Helena, the British army could look forward to a period of inactivity and, inevitably, reductions in manpower. Roderick and the 23rd Light Dragoons remained on the continent until the end of 1815, returning to Dover on Christmas Eve. Roderick spent Christmas Day 1815 on the march to Chichester, which his regiment eventually reached on New Year's Day. We know little of his activities over the next two years, although early in 1817 he seems to have fallen ill. His father told the parish priest in May that 'Roderick has been dangerously ill but thank God he has been better for some little time and is now at Cheltenham in a convalescent state'. He returned to his regiment and remained on active service (though they were doing very little) until 1818, when he went on half-pay. This perhaps suited his changing circumstances, for on 20 June 1818 Roderick married Isabella Brownlow, daughter of Lieutenant Colonel Charles (Baron) Brownlow of Lurgan, County Armagh. Isabella was four or five years older than Roderick, the wrong side of thirty, but his father was delighted with the match: 'The father has a large fortune (15,000 a year), the portion is not large (6,000) but there is a prospect of more. Her elder brother is Member for Armagh.'

Nevertheless, when Roderick took the opportunity to return to active duty and full-time pay in 1819, it was his father the Colonel who found the money to purchase what must have been an expensive commission in the 1st Life Guards. He later recorded that between 1813 and 1819 he spent £10,685 purchasing commissions for his son. Roderick had been touring Italy in the spring of 1819 but he returned to take up appointment as Captain in the Life Guards on 19 July. Purchasing a commission of the same rank as he had held in the 23rd Dragoons, but in one of the army's most prestigious units, can only be seen as a career-move for a man who was perhaps thinking seriously about pursuing a life-time career in the army.

25. The funeral of Caroline of Brunswick, estranged wife of George IV, which led to the riot at Knightsbridge barracks on Sunday 26 August, of which Roderick wrote an account.

The Life Guards were stationed in the capital at Knightsbridge barracks, and at this time they were mainly involved in ceremonial duties. Occasionally something a little more demanding was asked of them and one such incident, involving Roderick, took place in 1821. In mid-August George IV's estranged wife, Caroline of Brunswick, had died. When her funeral took place there were riots among her many supporters among the populace of London, during which two of the rioters were killed. They in turn were buried on Sunday 26 August. According to Mrs Arbuthnott's famous Journal 'there was a great riot at the Knightsbridge Barracks at the funeral of the two men... The people hissed and hooted at the soldiers and at last attacked one who was amongst them unarmed. His comrades defended him and a general battle ensued'. As it happened, Captain Roderick Macneil was on duty that day, and in the National Archives one can read his account of his own part in the event, which he wrote for his commanding officer.

My attention was arrested by a violent uproar in the Barracks Yard... I hastened to the spot and found one of our trumpeters bleeding on the ground... three men riding on the footpath were at the head of this rabble... I seized the bridle of the person's horse who appeared to me to be the most troublesome... I saw you rush out with several officers and heard you order the men instantly into barracks, which order was happily most promptly obeyed.

This was almost certainly Roderick's last action with the 1st Life Guards, for by the end of the month he had purchased a commission as a Major with the 84th (Yorks and Lancashire) Regiment of Foot. The move seems to have been purely to gain promotion, for only four months later on 29 December, he transferred regiment again, quickly returning to the cavalry, but now as a Major in the 2nd Life Guards. He was able to make this advantageous move by exchanging with Major Sir Charles Webb Dance who had actually served alongside him in the 23rd Light Dragoons at Waterloo. Within a month of taking up this commission his army rank was advanced brevet to Lieutenant Colonel, so Roderick's army career was suddenly looking very promising.

The same could not really be said for his father's estate on Barra. In recent years the Colonel had been pursuing 'improvements' on his estate. Some of these were undoubtedly beneficial both to the proprietor and to his tenants. Money was spent on road-building, trees were planted on the east side of the island, and some of the land on the Eoligarry home farm was improved with drainage schemes. The Barra fishermen had become among 'the most active and industrious in Scotland... their boats being large and well found compared with all others in the Western Isles'.

But these improvements came at a price. The success of the fisheries encouraged Macneil to create new, small crofts on the edge of the sea, incapable of supporting themselves from the land alone. The boom in the kelp industry during the Napoleonic wars had precisely the same effect, and also boosted the crofters' income. This in turn encouraged Macneil to raise his rents and the crofters to have larger families. But as MacCulloch noted in 1816 'everything capable of arable farming is already in cultivation', and new crofts could only be created right on the coast or on marginal land at best capable of producing potatoes. So existing crofts became overpopulated as cottars squatted alongside their kinfolk, and people grew ever more dependent on the potato. By 1811, 80 per cent of the islanders' nourishment came from potatoes.

The Colonel was determined to press ahead with further reforms, however, and in the summer of 1818 offered permanent leases to those tenants who would clear and enclose their land. There was resistance from the crofters and in December the Colonel wrote to the parish priest warning 'I will use every exertion that the land, and hay, are permanently divided: those for and against it will show me who I must look to and who not'. Relations between the Chief and his clansmen were clearly deteriorating, a fact which the Colonel himself recognized and lamented during an episode of emigration in 1816–17. At that time his protestations to priest Angus Macdonald still carried echoes of the old obligations of the Chief to his people:

(6 June 1816) It is no doubt distressing to my feelings that people to whom I am so much attached should leave me: but if it was for their good I should regret it less.

(25 June 1816) They cannot but believe me more ready to serve them for love, than Mr Fraser. (the emigration agent)

(8 August 1816) I am hurt that any man in Barra should want confidence in me... their suspicions are so revolting to me... I have at all times been willing to come forward for the protection of the people of Barra.

Nevertheless the Chief's appeal to his people had fallen on deaf ears in 1817 and 300 men, women and children left Barra and sailed on the *William Tell* to find new lives in Nova Scotia. Angus Macdonald, who must have been aware of the planned emigration, had never mentioned it to Macneil, and in the following year seems to have acted as an intermediary between the crofters and the emigration agent. Four years later another 350 Barra people left on the *Harmony*, again bound for Nova Scotia and Cape Breton.

It is not clear why so many decided to leave their homeland at this time, but their decision was probably influenced by several factors. First, the emigration agents, and Simon Fraser in particular, were active in the Western Isles at this time and were making would-be emigrants attractive offers. In the case of the *William Tell*, even the government appears to have offered some encouragement. Second, Barra itself was getting dangerously overcrowded. Between 1801 and 1821, despite losing more than 1,000 people to emigration, Barra's population rose from 1,900 to 2,300 people. New crofts for the growing population could only be provided on poor land incapable of supporting the tenants. Thirdly, the price of kelp was dropping and with it the cash that crofters could earn to pay their rent and buy a few luxuries was drying up. Quite simply, the prospects in Nova Scotia looked much better than those in Barra.

But in addition to all of this there was the changing and deteriorating relationship between Macneil and his kinsmen and tenants. Despite his possibly genuine protestations of concern for them, they were

26. Toxteth Park, Liverpool, where Roderick's father lived out his final days and died in April 1822.

increasingly regarded as part of the economic equation rather than part of the social fabric. And the Chief was growing increasingly isolated from them physically as well as emotionally and socially. His business trips to Liverpool seem to have eventually turned into temporary and then permanent residence there. In 1805 he wrote to Barra from Chester, and in 1809 from Prospect Place on the northern fringe of Liverpool. By 1810 he was enough of a resident to be listed in the local directory as 'Gentleman' living in Brownlow Street. In 1814 he was similarly described as a resident of Mount Vernon Street. Both streets were occupied mainly by merchants. By now his eldest (and illegitimate) daughter Catherine had married a Liverpool merchant, James Macdonald, who became a close friend of Macneil. Eventually, around 1816, he purchased a house in the then semi-rural Toxteth Park.

His letters to Angus Macdonald always express much interest in the affairs of Barra and its people, and as late as 1818 they still talk of him coming 'home'. But if such visits took place they seem to have been increasingly infrequent and short, although some of his siblings still lived in Barra House. With son and heir, Roderick, away at the wars and then travelling on the continent, the link between clansmen, homeland and Chief was becoming increasingly tenuous. When the Colonel died at home in Toxteth on Wednesday 24 April 1822, it was hanging by a thread.

6

'I was literally tied to the stake': Roderick Becomes Chief

When Roderick succeeded to the Chieftainship of the Clan Macneil, and the Lairdship of Barra, in April 1822 he was particularly ill-equipped for the task that faced him. The estate was beset with problems, but Roderick had little or no knowledge or experience of either farming or commercial matters. Neither did he have any experience of handling 2,000 crofters and fishermen who still believed that their ancestral laird was to some extent responsible for their well-being. Roderick's experience of managing people was the experience of an officer in the early nineteenth-century army – where officers issued orders and men obeyed them or faced a severe flogging or worse. Furthermore the hardship and deprivation faced by the crofters and cottars of Barra, dreadful as they were, hardly compared to the starvation and death from exposure and exhaustion that Roderick had witnessed in the retreat to Corunna, the agonizing deaths and permanent disablement suffered by thousands on the Walcheren expedition, or the carnage of Waterloo. His military experiences as a young man must have given Roderick a hard edge and perhaps a degree of indifference to suffering which would not have made him overly sympathetic to the plight of his tenants and kinsmen. Indeed, he probably knew little about the problems facing the crofters on Barra in 1822, since there is no evidence, and little reason to believe, that Roderick had set foot on the island since he joined the army in 1808. He and his kinsmen must have been virtually strangers when he returned to the island in December 1823.

Prior to this, Roderick had spent whatever time and attention his on-going army duties allowed him since his father's death in April, in trying to actually take control of the estate. The problem was that,

72

possibly unknown to him, his father in May 1820 had taken out a Deed of Probate which entrusted the estate of Barra (and his other lands in Knapdale) to twelve trustees. The nominated trustees were a mixture of family, Liverpool business friends, and Scottish lawyers. Roderick the Gentle's purpose in setting up this Trust was stated to be 'laying down and directing a mode of management which after mature deliberation I think most proper for clearing off progessively such debts as here after might endanger... the said estate'. And debts there certainly were. When he died, Roderick the Gentle owed around £30,000 – a large sum of money in those days and much of this debt was in the form of heritable bonds against the estate.

The Deed of Probate gave extensive powers to the Trustees. They could appoint the factor for the estate and thereby control the way in which it was run. They took the rent income, could sell part or all of the estate, and they could sell the colonel's moveable property, to pay off the debts and to secure annuities. These included £200 a year settled on each of Roderick's four unmarried sisters, and two other annuities for relatives totalling £70. The Trustees were to be the minors' tutors and curators. Roderick's younger brother Ewan was to be given a settlement of £5,000! Only when all debts had been paid and the annuities secured, could whatever then remained of the estate be handed over to Roderick. Meanwhile, furthermore, the Trustees were to act as sole executors and the colonel's 'own nearest of kin' were explicitly debarred from holding such office. Finally, the Trustees were given the power to ignore any challenge to their control from the new Macneil.

Although the Deed of Probate was no doubt set up with the best of intentions, it also seemed to carry the message that the Colonel did not trust his son and heir either to successfully run the estate or look after his younger siblings. Or perhaps the Colonel just felt that given Roderick's active service with the Life Guards, he was in no position to take on either responsibility. Roderick, understandably, had other views. In his earliest surviving letter to the parish priest, Angus Macdonald (October 1823), he rails against 'the ruinous nature of the Deeds executed by my late father' and says 'I was literally tied to the stake, having no alternative but to reduce them or consign myself and my family to penury'. He had tried, he told the priest, to negotiate a satisfactory solution to the situation in which he found himself but 'in those of whom, from near connection, I had a right to expect justice, if nothing more, I found only duplicity'. This was a broadside aimed at his siblings, particularly his younger brother Ewan, and his aunts. By now he had given up any hope of settling the matter by discussion and arbitration and had determined to seek legal redress.

In November 1823 he issued a Summons of Reduction against all possible claimants on the Estate of Barra – a list of no less than thirty-four persons, headed by his own daughter (an infant) and by his brother. Among the others named were sisters, aunts and uncles and their offspring, and all twelve trustees. Needless to say, the Summons was vigorously contested. Allegedly on the advice of two of the Trustees, Duncan Macneil and Patrick Robertson (advocates),

27. The beginning of the summons of reduction, by which Roderick sought to seize control of his father's estate. The summons was taken out against no less than thirty-four named individuals!

Roderick had gone to Barra in December 'to take possession as the Trust Deed was at an end'. He had appointed a factor and someone to supervise the kelping, and had sent various provisions for the inhabitants. In January 1824 Roderick had offered terms to the Trustees, which they appeared to have accepted but then prevaricated about. In June 1824 he wrote urging them to stick to the agreement he thought they had come to in January. Two weeks later he wrote again, his patience wearing thin, and threatened to withdraw from the agreed settlement unless it was concluded immediately. The Trustees' minutes reveal that Roderick's sisters had agreed to the terms, but his brother Ewan was still refusing them. He wanted £5,000 to be paid to him by 1830, all arrears owed to the sisters to be paid immediately, and that all legal costs should be borne by Roderick. The Trustees effectively decided to leave Roderick and Ewan to wrangle between themselves. The legal tussle dragged on interminably, and it was not until February 1826 – nearly four years after his father died, that Roderick finally took back full possession of the estate of Barra.

The legal uncertainty must have had some effect on Roderick's attempts to put the estate on a sounder financial footing, although as we have seen, he had already returned to Barra 'to take possession' and had appointed his own factor in December 1823. But beyond the legal restraints, Roderick was also hampered by his own ignorance of the true state of things in Barra, of Barra's limitations and potential for economic improvement, and of the wider economic circumstances of the time. As a result, his first attempts at turning the estate's finances around were both inept and of marginal financial significance. He decided that he could increase the productivity of his tenants if they worked harder and in his second letter to Angus Macdonald he demanded 'a great diminution in the number of holidays'. He repeated the demand two months later, this time with a clearly stated threat: 'If I don't experience <u>real</u> and <u>effectual</u> cooperation from the Bishop and yourself, I will bring in <u>Protestant tenants</u>.'
In the same letter he takes up two more themes which were to dominate his early attempts to make the estate more profitable – fishing and rents.

His complaints against the fishermen were two-fold. First that they wasted valuable time by themselves taking their catch to Glasgow to sell at whatever price 'the huxters choose to give', and second that many fishermen were in the habit of bartering their catch with passing ships for 'inferior and dear tobacco'. Ostensibly, Roderick was concerned in both cases that the fishermen were being ripped off, but of course his real complaint was that the fishermen were by-passing the landlord in selling their catch. And this is made clear in the same letter where he accused them not only of spending their money rather than paying the rent due to him, but providing shelter and food for cottars 'who are fed and housed on my land and pay me not a shilling'.

Initially his response to the fishermen was to threaten them with eviction if they continued these practices – 'they shall never again eat a potato on my property' – but also to supply them with new tackle. At the same time he set about trying to collect rent arrears, and provided tools and materials for improving the primitive roads on the island. His other initiative was to consider renting out his 'home' farm at Eoligarry to a lowland farmer, an indication perhaps that he did not himself envisage returning to live on Barra. These measures were all rather piecemeal and proved ineffective, partly because some were difficult to implement, partly because they were of little economic value, and partly because the factor, Mr MacLeod, seems to have been no match for either the crofters or the priest.

Roderick had recognized that Angus Macdonald was perhaps the key to success or failure, telling him plainly in a letter of 20 March 1824 'possessing as you do unbounded influence over your flock, I look to you for the most cordial cooperation'. His early letters to Macdonald regularly emphasized his goodwill towards the priest, and in July 1824 he reassured Macdonald: 'I will take care of your interest', adding conspiratorially, 'You understand that what I shall do for you is quite between ourselves'.

But Angus Macdonald's interests were very different from those of the Macneil, and even in the early letters from Roderick there are hints of his exasperation with the priest's constant excuses for the lack of cooperation from the tenants. What Roderick didn't know was that, just as in his father's time (in 1817), Macdonald was involved in encouraging the emigration of Catholic tenants from Barra. The threat of emigration is first mentioned by Macneil in a letter of 7 February 1825, who says that those who opposed changes to the way the estate was run 'held out emigration *in terrorum* – others again, to my knowledge, encouraged Mr McNiven (an emigration agent) with the view of introducing Protestants into the shoes of the deluded Roman Catholics'. Roderick makes his position clear: 'I have little dread of emigration. I certainly shall in all the various ways in my power oppose it.' By the end of July he had had enough of emigration threats, and of non-compliance with his orders concerning both fishing and kelping. On 30 July he sat down in the writing room of his comfortable London town house at 34 Montague Square, Marylebone, and penned what he himself termed a 'Proclamation'. Macdonald was to read it to his congregation 'the very first Sunday after receipt'. The Proclamation read:

1st.
You will tell the kelpers that they have earned my utmost displeasure. They have not obeyed my orders – nor the orders of those by me set over them, which I consider as disrespectful to me, as it is disgraceful to them. However, as they have worked, so shall they be paid.

2nd.
Say to the fishermen that their audacity and base ingratitude has quite disgusted me. That if they do not within eight and forty hours after this proclamation, bend their energies to the daily prosecution of their calling as fishermen, I shall turn every man of them off the island were they steeped to their ears in debt – tell them also that since they have shown themselves so unworthy of that interest, which in my heart I felt for them, I shall follow out my plans without in the most trifling degree consulting their feelings or prejudices.

3rdly.

Say to those who are about to emigrate that I sincerely wish them well through it, and assure those who have signed and repented that their repentance comes too late – So help me God, they shall go, at all events off my property, man, woman and child. Tell the people once for all, that I shall consider any act of inattention to the orders of my factor Mr Stewart as an impertinence to myself. Nor shall any one who dares even to hesitate to obey him and Mr Parry (in both of whom I have the greatest confidence) remain on my property should his, or their character been even so good previously. Lastly I shall exert myself to the utmost to crush all the disreputable trafficking and smuggling which has been too long tolerated.

R.MacNeil

The uncompromising language of the Proclamation left no doubt as to what Macneil expected of his tenants, nor of his exasperation with their response to his demands. It spelt out with equal clarity what would be the penalty for non-compliance – eviction and exile. But there was another dimension to Macneil's attitude to his kinsmen which came out more clearly in the letter which accompanied the Proclamation – quite simply, he despised them. They 'cannot be depended upon from their fickleness, idleness and stiff-necked prejudice' Macneil told Macdonald. In another letter a few months earlier he had told the priest that the islanders suffered from 'inveterate sloth and pig-headedness'. In a letter sent a week after the Proclamation, he laid claim to 'old feudal feelings' but any such feelings were entirely one-sided. His people were there to show unswerving loyalty and obedience, but he seems to have recognized no obligations to them in return. Again, the letter which accompanied the Proclamation spelt out quite clearly Macneil's view of his relationship with his kinsmen and tenants. 'If one set of servants (tenants at will are nothing else) won't do, the master must try others': not laird and kinsmen, but master and servants.

Macneil had by now also got wise to Angus Macdonald's duplicity. His early letters to the priest had not only asked for his support

28. Roderick's house at 34 Montagu Square, Marylebone, from which he issued his notorious 'Proclamation' to his tenants on 30 July 1826.

and offered him (undisclosed) favours in return, but had proffered the hand of friendship: 'You are the only person connected with my property, from whom I have experienced a friendly disposition during the time it was in other hands, this I cannot easily forget' (20 March 1824).

A year later he reveals some irritation with the priest's meddling: 'it was quite unnecessary to urge him (the factor) to represent to me anything on the subject' and 'your apprehensions were groundless as well as the implied neglect on my part' (15 March 1825). By the time of the Proclamation he was sick and tired of the priest urging him to make more concessions: 'Abandon all ideas of further condescensions (as you term it) on my part to your spoilt children' (30 July 1825). A week later Macneil wrote again to Macdonald because 'It is desirable you should know my sentiments very distinctly'. After rehearsing how he had looked to the priest for assistance and had apparently been assured of his good offices, he said he now realized he had been misled. 'Either you are not free from prejudice yourself, or your feelings lead you to encourage it in others.' His suspicions were well-founded, for Macdonald seems to have been heavily involved in the plans for a second mass emigration, to the extent that he held money for some of the would-be emigrants, and had powers of attorney given to him by emigrant groups. Proof positive of Macdonald's pivotal role in promoting a mass emigration at this time comes from a letter from John Chisholm, priest on neighbouring South Uist, written to Macdonald in August 1826. Here, only weeks after 200–300 people had left the island for Cape Breton, Chisholm refers plainly to 'the ferment you left, and perhaps fermented among them' (i.e. the emigrants). But by this time, Macdonald had himself left the island, mysteriously elevated to the rectorship of the prestigious Scots College in Rome.

Just as a change of priest took place at this time, so Macneil for the second time replaced his factor. The new factor's name – Mr Stewart – appears in both the Proclamation and the letter which accompanied it. He took up his position probably in April of 1825, and there is good reason to think that he may have been at least partly responsible for the tough tone and hard line which Roderick adopted a few months later. 'Mr Stewart' was Alexander Stewart who later became factor of Scourie on the west coast of Scotland, and a close friend of the notorious enforcer of highland clearances Patrick Sellar. Writing to Sellar in 1840, Stewart described the strategy to develop the estate of Barra, which he had placed before Macneil in 1825.

'My plan to Colonel Macneil was to remove hordes of small tenantry from the west to the east side so as to get at the most valuable of the pasture for stock and to put down fishing settlements on the south and east for the purpose of putting employment at fishing ling and cod within reach of the great part of the population.' Stewart said that Macneil thought the plan to be a good one and began to implement it.

This appears to be the case. Apart from serious efforts to get the fishing industry productive and contributing to the estate's coffers, up until mid-1825 Macneil and his factors had really only tinkered at the edges with the estate's management. The new factor had a clear and far-ranging vision of what was required to turn the estate into a profitable business and he appears to have sold that vision to Roderick. On the west coast a name-sake of the Laird, Roderick Macneil of Grean, later claimed that it was about 1825–6 that he was evicted and his house burned. 'All the lands of the townland… were given to the lowland farmer beside us,' he recalled. In autumn 1827, the new priest Neil Macdonald wrote to his predecessor telling him that 'McStuart' had unroofed 'all the houses in the west-side townships of Borve, Tangusdale and Allasdale'. At the same time the east coast townships seem to have seen a marked influx of crofters, the six townships from Bruernish to Brevig seeing an increase over the next ten years from thirty-three tenants to seventy-five. The lands on the east were notably unsuitable for almost any kind of cultivation apart from small plots for potatoes, and the appearance of new blackhouses strung around the bleak coast of Bruernish confirms that the new tenancies were expected to be maintained mainly from fishing activity. To sweeten the pill, in 1827 Roderick made the fishermen 'very fair offers about their fishing, which they accepted', though Chisholm noted wryly: 'I doubt much they will be inclined to implement their part of the bargain.'

The drive to make the fishing more productive, however, was primarily focussed on the south coast at Castlebay. Here Macneil planned to establish a 'fishing village', which is first mentioned in the last of the letters to Angus Macdonald, written in October 1825. The construction of the village, with a road suitable for carts, seems to have progressed well enough for Roderick to write to the factor of Mackenzie of Seaforth in 1826 'to learn if any of your tenants can be induced to establish themselves in my fishing village'. It may be that this initiative was undertaken not just because of a shortage of 'volunteers' from amongst the dispossessed crofters from the west coast townships but also because Macneil, probably under Stewart's

29. Potatoes growing on lazybeds on Barra. Small plots like these were cultivated wherever there was sufficient soil by the tenants on the east coast crofts.

30. The ruins of a blackhouse on the east coast of Bruernish, one of many built by tenants evicted from their west coast crofts who were leased new tenancies on this bleak and barren stretch of coast.

prompting, thought there was more productivity to be gained by fishing the further banks. The fishermen of Barra had traditionally exploited only the nearer banks, and would need to be taught new skills. Evidence later given to the Select Committee on Emigration confirmed that 'Macneil brought fishermen from Peterhead to teach the people the art of deep-sea fishing'.

Stewart's strategy, which was essentially to raise higher and more reliable rents from farms on the west side of the island, supplemented by additional rents from the new small tenancies on the east and south coast, together with a substantial increase in income from fishing, was in place by mid-summer 1826. But the emigration of 200–300 people in August of that year immediately put the plan in jeopardy, with the loss of both rental income and labour. New tenants were sought from neighbouring areas and in October 1827 Neil Macdonald wrote that 'North Uist and Tiree people are daily flocking in', bringing to pass Macneil's threat of 1824 that he would bring in Protestant tenants. As a Protestant himself, it would have troubled Macneil not at all.

By this time, too, he had yet another factor – Alexander Stewart had gone. According to Stewart, Macneil 'had neither capital nor perseverance' to push through his strategy to a successful conclusion. Whether Macneil grew disillusioned with Stewart or vice-versa is not clear, but they parted company. Macneil, perhaps shaken by the scale of the emigration in 1826, and perhaps finding no takers for the new west coast farms, appears to have reversed his policy of clearing these townships. The estate was still in a perilous position, and Roderick was desperately searching for a way to save it.

7

'A large and expensive works': The Industrial Revolution Comes to Barra

Alexander Stewart's plan for Barra was focussed exclusively on developing the fishing and pastoral economy of the island. Kelp production had no part in it, probably because Stewart could see little prospect of the industry ever recovering the economic significance it had in the early years of the nineteenth century. During the Napoleonic wars in particular, with access cut off to Spanish barilla, Hebridean kelp (processed seaweed) had become the prime source of alkali for glass and soap manufacturers. The price of made kelp rose steadily through the first decade of the century, from about £10 per ton to a peak of around £20 a ton in 1810. Thereafter the price fell back, and with the defeat of Napoleon and the re-opening of the Spanish barilla market, the price fell below the £10 mark by 1820. Between 1822 and 1830 the Government reduced and/or abolished the duty on all of the major competitors to kelp: barilla, salt, pot and pearl ashes, and sulphur. Most significant of all, in 1823 the so-called 'Leblanc process' for producing alkali from salt was introduced in Liverpool. This promised to make available large quantities of alkali at low prices and with little or no transportation costs to the soap and glass manufacturers of Liverpool and Manchester. By 1825 when Roderick appointed Stewart as factor on Barra the price was already down to about £4–5 a ton and the future of kelp manufacture looked increasingly bleak.

Roderick, with his Liverpool connections, would have been aware of the 'Leblanc process' as well as the competition from other materials, but the kelping tradition was particularly strong on Barra. During the last few years of his father's life, the island was exporting about 300 tons of made kelp a year, and between 1817 and 1821 kelping contributed a net profit of over £6,300 to the estate's economy. Roderick clearly believed it could still make a valuable contribution to his income, and he berated the kelpers for their disobedience to his orders in his Proclamation of July 1825.

While kelping activity took a back-seat during the factorship of Stewart, as soon as he had left Barra Macneil's thoughts again turned to the possibility of reviving the industry's flagging fortunes. Indeed, it is possible that Macneil's commitment to kelping may have hastened or even initiated Stewart's departure. In his letter to Patrick Sellar, Stewart links Macneil's lack of perseverance with Stewart's plans for farms and clearance to his having made the acquaintance of 'a Welsh chemist'. This chemist, whose name we do not know, persuaded Macneil that he had a chemical process which could greatly enhance the alkali content of made kelp. He was one of several entrepreneurs at this time who were aware that the highland proprietors were desperately seeking ways to revive their kelp income. Mr Mccrummen of Leith had experimented in 1822 to find ways to increase the alkali content of kelp by using better kelp kilns and by stricter control of the process. In 1830 Clanranald employed Mccrummen and Dr John Anderson to carry out trials on Uist, but they failed to yield any improvements.

Roderick Macneil was ahead of them, however, both in time and ambition. In July 1828 we get the first intimation of what was afoot on Barra. Parish priest Neil Macdonald reported to his predecessor that the Macneil 'now means to set up a glass and soap factory at Bahierva (Northbay). The bricks etc are already on the shore'. As all subsequent records make abundantly clear, the works were not to make soap or glass, but to process kelp to produce higher quality soda ashes and alkali, but even today the tradition is alive on Barra that the factory was for glass making. Construction work appears to have been slow or delayed, however, and in January 1830 Macdonald reported that the factory would 'in course of the spring, if well, be fit for work'. In March he was able to tell Angus Macdonald that 'the works at Bahierva are now complete', but putting them into operation seems to have been as cumbersome a process as building them.

In 1832, Duncan Shaw, factor on the Clanranald estate on Uist wrote: 'It is not at present very easy to judge the success of the scheme... another season will inform us whether the plan is worth following or not.' As late as 1835 a report prepared for Colonel Gordon of Cluny said that Macneil had 'commenced in 1830 or 1831, completing only these past few months, a large and expensive works for the manufacture of alkali or soda ashes from kelp'. Since Macneil had begun to purchase quantities of kelp from Clanranald in 1833, it seems the factory was in production by this time, and Duncan Shaw reported in August that the works were in full operation. But a gradual build up towards full production seems to be indicated by the quantities of Clanranald kelp Macneil purchased in 1833–35, 55 tons, 387 tons and 537 tons respectively. In all, the factory had taken seven years from the initial purchase of building materials to a point where it could perhaps begin to produce significant quantities of the enhanced kelp products and provide Macneil some return on his investment.

That investment was clearly a very substantial one indeed. Later records show that in this period Macneil took on further loans to add to the burden of debt he was already carrying from his father's time. Between 1829 and 1833 he borrowed £10,000 from the Westminster Insurance Office, £7,000 from George Gardner of Manchester, and £8,000 from Colonel Maxwell Close. But the biggest creditor was a Liverpool entrepreneur, Harold Littledale. Littledale was a remarkable young man. Known in his youth as being 'the best amateur boxer in the north of England' he joined his family firm as a seventeen-year-old apprentice. His commercial abilities were such that at the age of twenty-five he became a partner in the company and quickly built a substantial fortune. He was only thirty when he began to invest in Macneil's factory, and his folly was remembered ever after in Liverpool. When he died at the age of eighty-six, his obituary in the Liverpool Mercury recalled that he had lost money 'helping a poor Scotchman to work a kelp invention in the Western Islands'! Gordon's report of 1835 said that Littledale had loaned Macneil 'large sums of money upon the security of the Barra alkali works', and records of 1836–37 reveal the loans to have been in the region of £30,000. In total the alkali works appear to have cost in excess of £50,000!

The Daily Post

THURSDAY, MARCH 14, 1839.

THE LATE HAROLD LITTLEDALE.

31. Harold Littledale of Liverpool, Roderick's biggest creditor who bankrolled Macneil's chemical factory to the tune of £30,000.

It may have been the need to seek out new sources of capital that slowed down the building of the works, but as the sums involved indicate, Macneil's alkali factory was built on an ambitious scale. Although most of the buildings in the complex were pulled down in the 1870s we can get some idea of the factory from its surviving structural remains (now part of the Catholic presbytery at Northbay) and the brief description of the works that was compiled in 1836. The factory stood on the south side of Northbay and was built to front directly onto the water. The whole complex was enclosed by a strong stone wall about 4m high and the frontage was 35m long and the sides 40m, with a main gateway on the west side. The north wall, fronting onto water, was pierced by no less than seven large, double-gated ports, the thresholds of which were set just above high water level. It was presumably through these gateways that made kelp was offloaded from the boats which brought it from Uist, directly into the interior of the factory. The barrels of enhanced soda ashes presumably went out through the same gateways to be shipped to Liverpool and Manchester, where the whole of Macneil's output is

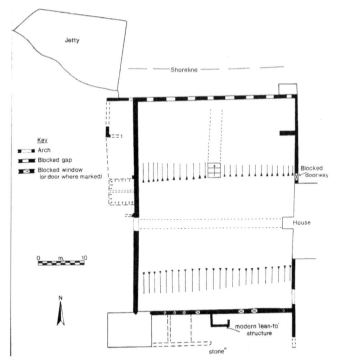

32. A plan of the surviving remains of Macneil's chemical factory at Northbay. Note the projecting jetty which allowed ships to be loaded and unloaded at low water.

33. The sea-wall of Macneil's chemical factory with its blocked double-gated portals for unloading ships bringing kelp from Uist, and loading ships taking the manufactured 'soda ashes' to the mainland.

said to have been sold. Outside the north-west corner of the factory a jetty or quay 20m by 10m was built, its interior filled with small boulders which were covered over with sand. This structure was built just above the low water mark, so that it was possible for boats to load and unload at the factory at both high and low water.

Inside the enclosing wall the interior appears to have been divided into three sections which ran across the building east to west. The central area was raised up above the level of the areas to north and south. At the west end, just inside the gateway was a furnace room with a tall brick chimney. Almost all traces of other internal structures have disappeared but the description of 1836 lists the various rooms and buildings which made up the complex. There was a Joiner's Shop, a Smithy, a Cooper's Shop, and various store-rooms including a 'Kelp House'. The focal point of the complex, however, were the rooms where the kelp was processed. These were described as the Mixing Room, the Carbonating Furnace Room, and the Crystallizing House. This suggests a three-stage process involving mixing of made kelp with chemicals, heating, and cooling. But the details of the process were, and remain, something of a mystery and there was much speculation about it among the proprietors and factors of other kelping estates at the time.

Equal uncertainty surrounded the economics of the factory. Macneil used both kelp made by his own tenants in Barra and kelp purchased from the Clanranald estate on Uist. He bought the Uist kelp at between £2 10s and £2 15s per ton. Just how much made kelp was needed to produce a ton of enhanced soda ashes was a secret, but according to Shaw 'some say as high as four tons'. The price which Macneil got for his improved ashes was also something of a mystery and appears to have varied, but was rumoured to be between £10 and £18 per ton. Allowing for manufacturing costs and transport, Macneil's profit margin was probably only significant when his product sold near the top of its price range. If Barra was producing its annual crop of 250–300 tons of made kelp, along with the 550 tons imported from Clanranald in 1835, then 200–250 tons of enhanced soda ashes may have been available to sell that year.

Macneil might have made an operating profit of between £800 and £1,500. Colonel Gordon, a hard-nosed businessman if ever there was, was quite impressed and offered the opinion that Macneil 'will in a short time succeed in relieving himself of his difficulties'. There was the prospect that profits might grow, since the factory was clearly built to produce on an industrial scale.

There was one further room listed in the 1836 description of the factory which perhaps reflects the industrial ambitions of its owner. It was labelled the Barrack Room, and since there is no suggestion (or reason why) a military unit might be based here the title may reflect the room's use as temporary accommodation for the work force. One contemporary report spoke of 500 islanders being employed in alkali production by Macneil. That is almost certainly an inflated figure, even assuming that most of these people were crofters who undertook seasonal kelping. But both the size and complexity of the works suggest a sizeable workforce at Northbay itself. The reason accommodation may have been provided for them, when one would expect most to have had blackhouse homes they could return to, is that some of the labour force at the factory may have been brought from Berneray. In Robert Stevenson's 1834 Report to the Commissioners for Northern Lights he mentions that the people of Berneray had been removed by Macneil, and he repeats the claim in 1835 and 1836, but now includes the population of Mingulay too. In total this may have been as many as 120 people, of whom perhaps a third or more would have been of working age. Recording the return of the people to Berneray in 1838 Stevenson reports that they had lived '3 or 4 years on Barra at the laird's kelp-works'. Whether the Mingulay people had worked there too is uncertain but seems quite possible. Macneil had apparently employed what can only be described as 'forced-labour', since the people cleared from Berneray (and probably Mingulay) had no choice but to take up residence at the kelp-works or be evicted and homeless. Macneil had brought the industrial revolution to Barra in an uncompromising way and the lot of the labour force at his factory was in many ways worse than that of the lowliest mill-hands in the Scottish lowlands.

The alkali factory impacted on almost every family on Barra, with crofters required to harvest kelp and supply peat fuel for the factory. We know from later records that during the kelping season even the young children were required to help with the kelping. At the same time the crofters were prevented from enriching their small and infertile potato and barley plots with seaweed, and were forced to give priority to kelping over working their land and herding their animals. Although they were paid for the kelp they produced, kelping wages had fallen along with the price of kelp, while rents had continued to increase. Rent arrears were widespread, and Roderick pursued the debtors with a zeal that his father had never displayed.

In October 1827 Neil Macdonald himself witnessed the aggressive new policy towards crofters with rent arrears: 'I have actually seen in this very farm cattle taken away by the factor and ground officers in a violent struggle.' After a brief respite, the cattle seizures began again and were worse than ever. Macdonald reported in 1831 that 'our great Laird thought it not sufficient to send a horde of ground officers and constables once or twice through the country in taking up cattle, horses etc, but must needs go himself at their head. The very calfs were demanded at last and hurried to Eoligarry.'

By now Roderick seems to have decided to focus his farming activities on cattle and sheep. Cattle seized from tenants were added to his own stock, and he was said to have 600 cattle grazing at Eoligarry at this time. He was alleged to have ordered the slaughter of all the sheep on Barra, except of course his own flock, which in 1836 numbered between 2,000 and 4,000 animals. He had by now abandoned all hope of making a profit from the fishing. He had fallen out with the fishermen again in 1828, the fishermen (as Father Chisholm had predicted) having reneged on their part of the deal with Macneil and resorted to bartering fish for provisions with passing ships. When the fishing bounty was phased out in 1830, Roderick washed his hands of the fishing.

He seems to have cultivated the priest Neil Macdonald, just as he had his predecessor. 'I have been frequently down with him. He seems uncommonly kind,' wrote Macdonald in 1828, and again in

1831, 'The Laird... treated me with more than usual kindness.' For his part, the priest seems to have thought that the errant laird was not beyond redemption: 'He would not be much behind his father was he to remain in the Country and not be so easily advised and that by people that never saw the property.'

Whether he made this point to Roderick himself is unknown, but Macneil certainly began to spend more time on Barra. Roderick was by now directly involved in the running of the estate and the commissioning of the alkali works. He had left active service with the Lifeguards in 1828 and gone on half pay, and by 1830 he and his wife had moved from London to Helensburgh, on the Firth of Clyde. From here he could more easily and frequently travel to Barra. Mrs Macneil and their young daughter Caroline went with him and they took up seasonal residence at Barra House, Eoligarry. At Eoligarry, Roderick and his family seem to have lived in some style. To look after their needs they employed a cook, a house maid, a house servant, a dairy maid and a kitchen maid as well as a groom and gardener. The home farm employed a further eighteen people, mostly labourers and herders, under the supervision of the factor. For the first time in perhaps nearly two decades, the Macneil of Barra was spending weeks, or even months, back on his ancestral island living among his kinsmen.

He was in residence at Barra House in January 1834 when the brig *Fleece*, on its way from Riga to Newry, was forced to seek shelter off the east coast of Barra. The ship's master, Captain Henderson, went ashore and was offered hospitality by Macneil. He was wined and dined at Eoligarry and given a bed for the night. Next day he took breakfast with Roderick, and then climbed the hill above the house to see how the sea was running and whether his ship was safe and sound. An hour later, a shepherd found the body of Captain Henderson lying at the foot of a cliff. Speculation that he had slipped and fallen was discounted when it was noted that there were no bruises on his body, and a doctor confirmed that death was due to 'apoplexy', presumably caused by a thrombosis. The steep climb up Ben Eoligarry and perhaps on to Ben Scurrival had proved too much for the Captain. Macneil arranged the captain's funeral, which according to one account, was 'respectably conducted'. The whole sad little episode revealed that Roderick could still show hospitality and humanity in his dealings with a reluctant visitor to his home.

Relations with his immediate family, however, were far from cordial. He had of course fallen out with his younger brother Ewan over the terms of his father's will, and had included Ewan and all of his sisters in the Summons of Reduction submitted in 1823. In 1827 he fell out with his uncle and principal tacksman, Donald Macneil of Vatersay. He apparently believed that his uncle had been actively involved in encouraging the emigrants who had left the island for Canada in 1826. Hugh Macneil, Donald's eldest son, reported that 'our family has left its native home being forced from the place by that monster of ingratitude, the Colonel'. It may be that Roderick threatened eviction, but did not go ahead with it, for when Donald Macneil died in 1830, his widow continued to live in the estate house on Vatersay. In 1836 she was reported as in possession of 'the house, garden and park, with grass of eight cows, two horses, four

34. The ruins of Donald Macneil's estate house on Vatersay, from which Roderick allegedly evicted his uncle's family. But Donald's widow was still there when Roderick went bankrupt in 1836.

sheep, rent free. Granted to her and any unmarried daughters in their lifetime by Macneil'. Hugh Macneil seems to have made some sort of peace with Roderick by the time of his father's death, opening a shop in Castlebay that year and taking the leases of the island's public houses, for which he was to pay Roderick £200 p.a.

Roderick's relations with his family were not that dissimilar to his relations with the parish priest and the Protestant minister. He entered into litigation with the Reverend Nicolson in 1827, and issued orders for Neil Macdonald to be evicted in 1828, but subsequently maintained cordial relations with both. One gets the impression of a man with a quick temper, acting on impulse, given to a change of heart shortly after. To some extent this behaviour may be explained by the pressures under which Roderick was operating in the period from 1822 to 1836. Inheriting an estate over which he had no legal control, and substantial debts and financial commitments, he had to devote most of his energies for three years to trying to overturn the terms of his father's will. He had little time or experience to devote to running the estate. He tried a succession of factors, some of whom were clearly incompetent, but quickly lost faith in each of them. Meanwhile, his tenants were neither able nor willing to carry out the 'improvements' he required. In 1826 he lost 300 of them to emigration, and in 1827 bad weather brought many of them to the brink of starvation. When he was offered the opportunity to invest in a new process to enhance kelp, he took the gamble and committed himself entirely to the venture. The size of the works, and of the investment required to build it, was on an industrial scale. In 1836, it looked as if the gamble might just pay off.

8

'His Majesty's rebel': Roderick Goes Bankrupt

On 28 September 1836 James Sinclair, Messenger at Arms, proceeded to the Market Cross in Edinburgh and having attracted the attention of passers-by with three 'Oyeahs', he loudly denounced Lieutenant Colonel Roderick Macneil 'His Majesty's rebel, and put him to the horn by three blasts thereof'. Two weeks later, the procedure was repeated at the Market Cross in Inverness. What had brought Roderick, a senior officer in King William's army with a distinguished service record, to such infamy?

Quite simply, he had failed to meet a demand issued by Colonel John Gordon of Cluny in July for the repayment (with interest) of a loan of £3,500. Gordon had not himself loaned Macneil the money but had 'bought' the debt in 1832. When a second demand was issued on 16 September and Roderick failed to pay up, then he was condemned to being 'horned and poigned'. The 'horning' carried out at the market crosses in Edinburgh and Inverness served as a public humiliation; the 'poigning' involved the seizure of all Macneil's moveable possessions as a first step to paying off the debt. The same day as the 'horning' a warrant was issued for the arrest and imprisonment of Roderick Macneil. Two weeks later, having tracked down Macneil to his temporary lodgings, Roderick Macdonald, Messenger at Arms, 'carefully searched all the apartments... in order to have apprehended and incarcerated the person of the said Lt Col R Macneil, but could not find him, he having absconded'.

The very next day, Macneil himself petitioned for his estate to be sequestered, the petition supported by his wine merchants, Messrs Bell Rennie of Leith, to whom he owed over £400, some of which had been outstanding since 1834. The size of this debt alone (in

35. The 'Mercat' Cross in Edinburgh where Roderick was publicly declared 'His Majesty's rebel' on 28 September 1836, having failed to pay his bills.

modern day terms, something like £30,000!) suggested that this might be the tip of a very large financial iceberg. And so it proved. As other creditors came forward so the unpaid bills mounted. Some were relatively small matters: £8 to a Glasgow bookseller, £14 to a London carpet maker, and £41 to George Wallis, his tailor in Edinburgh. Other bills were more substantial: £126 to his bootmaker, George Hobey of London, £327 to George Walker, Grocer, and £337 to Jack Patterson, Upholsterer, both of Glasgow. While it was certainly not unknown for a gentleman to be slow in paying his tailor, his bootmaker and his grocer, the size of these bills suggest they had gone unpaid for some time. A bill for £68 from the Royal Hotel Edinburgh had first been lodged in 1830! There were other personal loans, including money from Harold Littledale, that were much larger. When all these personal debts were added up they eventually totalled £49,000.

The personal debts, however, were more than matched by heritable bonds taken out to finance the estate and latterly the chemical works. These included bonds to the value of £31,400 taken out and 'bequeathed' to him by his father. To these he had added new debts totalling another £29,500, some from individuals such as George Gardner of Manchester, and others from companies such as the Westminster Insurance Office. With interest these various bonds now totalled a debt burden of over £66,000, making a total debt of at least £115,000 – or in today's terms, something approaching £10 million!

Against these debts, Roderick could assemble very little by way of assets. His bank account held £1,564, his personal effects were estimated to be worth a paltry £1,500, and the chemical works perhaps £2,000. His only other asset was the estate itself, which was optimistically estimated to be worth £85,000. When presented with these figures, Macneil said he thought they were about right, and claimed that in August of 1836 he had been offered £75,000 for the estate.

The Trustees appointed to administer the sequestered estate, to sell the assets, and pay off the creditors, set to work with some optimism, under the chairmanship of Edinburgh lawyer Charles Murray Barstow. They appointed a new agent and factor for the estate, Charles Shaw, and sent him off to Barra with a servant and two officers in the bleak weather of October 1836. His first task would be to make an inventory both of the estate and its animal stock, and of the contents of Barra House. Shaw seems to have been a sensible and decent man. He told the Trustees that he 'went to Barra fully aware of the delicacy and difficulty of the task I had undertaken, with every wish to show the Colonel the greatest courtesy and respect and to go through the business in the way most agreeable to his feelings'.

He arrived on a Sunday and went straight to Barra House. Here, the difficulty of his task was made very plain to him by an irate Macneil who berated him for having arrived without giving notice of his coming. 'I will not be ridden over roughshod,' said Roderick, and then went on to say that he was not yet ready to co-operate in the inventory taking, and that Shaw should simply go away and come back in eight or ten days time. Shaw pointed out that at this time of year that was not a practical option, and Macneil then said he was willing to discuss the matter further. They talked and negotiated for more than two hours, at the end of which Roderick in a sudden *volte face* said that Shaw could commence work the very next day. It was agreed that he should begin by taking an inventory of the sheep that Macneil grazed on Vatersay, the neighbouring island to the south. Shaw perhaps felt a little better disposed to Macneil.

But as he was leaving Barra House Shaw was anonymously informed that at that very moment a certain Michael Maceachern of Arisaig was loading fifty-five cattle on board ship down at the Eoligarry jetty – less than half a mile from where he stood. This put new meaning on Macneil's assertion that he 'wasn't ready' for Shaw, and perhaps explained why he had upbraided Shaw at length and then held him in conversation for upwards of three hours. He immediately confronted Macneil, who assured him that the cattle had been sold to Maceachern earlier in the year, before sequestration, and had simply been grazing at Eoligarry until Maceachern could arrange their shipping to the mainland. Shaw would have none of it, and said that the animals must be immediately unloaded. Macneil argued and prevaricated, and by the time Shaw had insisted the animals be taken off the ship, he found the ship had already sailed.

On the Monday morning Shaw set off to take an inventory of the sheep that Macneil kept on Vatersay, the neighbouring island to the south. Trekking south to Castlebay, Shaw records that: 'On my way to the ferry I was informed that nearly 200 head of cattle had been ferried over from Vatersay the previous day and that they were somewhere among the hills.' Vatersay was a smaller island and its terrain much less easily used to hide animals. Shaw's servant, who by chance had taken a short cut over the hills, said that he had seen a large drove of cattle. Shaw dispatched an officer to search for them, but on his return from Vatersay he was told that the animals were now dispersed among the many crofters. Again, Shaw confronted Macneil and again Macneil said that these animals, too, had been sold to Maceachern back in the summer. Shaw didn't believe a word of it, and Roderick then attempted to strike a deal. Perhaps, said

Macneil, if Shaw took fifty or sixty of the animals, the rest could be allowed to be sent off to Arisaig. But Shaw stood firm and seized all the animals. By now he was well aware that he was dealing with a cunning and resourceful opponent.

On 28 October, having completed an inventory of the sheep and cattle on the estate Shaw turned his attention to Barra House. Every item, however insignificant, in each of the two dozen rooms and outbuildings was listed. The drawing room contained '1 fender, 2 baskets, 3 boxes and a trunk'. In Macneil's bedroom Shaw found a bedstead, a table, 2 chairs, and a basin stand. There was not a cupboard or a chest of drawers to be found in the bedrooms of Macneil, his wife or his daughter. Most rooms seemed sparsely furnished and there were no carpets on the floors. The pantry was equipped with a lot of crockery and cutlery, but the pottery was of average quality, the cutlery of base metals, and there was no crystal. All in all it was hardly what one expected in the mansion of either the proprietor of a Highland estate or the home of an officer and a gentleman.

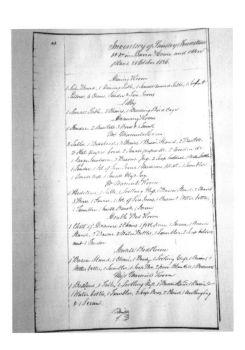

36. Part of the inventory of Barra House, prepared by Charles Shaw for the Trustees. It is notable for the sparsity of furniture and personal belongings, which were later revealed to have been shipped out by Macneil to escape seizure.

Before he left Barra, Shaw had stumbled on the explanation. When he went to make an inventory of the chemical works on 7 November he found little of value or interest there – mainly tools and containers for processed kelp. But once again someone whispered in his ear, and in a nearby blackhouse he discovered four crates full of furniture. His informer told him that they had been hidden in the chemical factory and moved into the blackhouse just before he took the inventory. Furthermore, he was told that more crates of furniture and other effects had been shipped off the island to Arisaig. In fact it seems likely that the chemical factory had been used as a 'clearing station' by Macneil because it had been designed to enable heavy loads to be easily put on board ships coming into the deep sheltered waters of Northbay.

Shaw took his leave of Macneil who, perhaps thinking he had got the better of Shaw, was all affability and told him that he was aware of his difficult situation and that he thought Shaw 'had done everything in the most agreeable and gentlemanly manner'. After Shaw had gone, Macneil resumed shipping more crate-loads of household goods to Arisaig. Further items seem to have been sent to Ireland with Macneil's wife, Isabella, who returned to stay for a while with her family in Armagh.

But Roderick's triumph was short-lived. Shaw had alerted the Sheriff's office at Inverness to the hijacked cattle and the reports of crate-loads of furniture having been sent to Arisaig. On 14 December a search warrant was issued, and the Sherrif's men turned up at Michael Maceachern's farm at Arisaig on 16 December and spent four days searching his property, as well as the sloop *Adelaide* anchored nearby, for good measure. The search revealed no less than seventy-one crates of personal effects hidden in Maceachern's loft. One was opened and found to contain seventy-eight pieces of china including some which had featured in the inventory taken in the pantry at Barra House! In addition to the seventy-one crates, the Sheriff's men also recovered two carpets, six chests of drawers, two tables, fourteen chairs and a pianoforte. All of these items were seized, along with the cattle shipped over in October, and were subsequently sold at auction to help meet the outstanding debts.

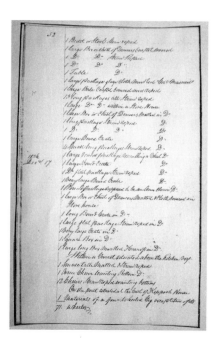

37. Part of the list of the seventy-one crates of personal belongings and more than two dozen items of furniture, the property of Roderick Macneil, discovered and seized by the sheriff's men in a barn at Arisaig.

Meanwhile, the Trustees had summoned Macneil to appear before them in Edinburgh on 8 December, to explain himself. When they met there was no Macneil, but a letter from his solicitor stating that the bad weather prevented the Colonel, who was still on Barra, from attending. Could the examination be postponed? Reluctantly the Trustees agreed. In January they received information that Macneil had resumed shipping property and livestock off the island but attempts to bring him to a meeting in Edinburgh again faltered when a letter arrived from Dr Macleod of Uist. 'I was called to visit the Colonel. He had for some time been indisposed. On my arrival I found the Colonel to be labouring under what I considered to be rheumatic gout.' The doctor went on to paint a pitiful picture of Roderick, with 'flying pains about his chest, swollen legs, not able to walk, emaciated'. Under the circumstances the Trustees agreed that they would defer Macneil's examination for a month. But once more he failed to turn up on the appointed day.

Just as bad weather was a plausible excuse for Roderick not taking passage across the Minches in December, so it is quite possible that he was suffering from gout (particularly in view of the enormous quantity of wine he had apparently bought and consumed over the previous twelve months!). But equally there can be little doubt that he made the best of the situation and took the opportunity to try and put more of his property beyond the reach of the Trustees. He could not hide at Eoligarry forever, however, and early in March 1837 he left Barra. As far as we know he never returned to the island home of the Clan Macneil.

He wrote to the Trustees from Glasgow on 11 March and agreed to attend an examination in Edinburgh on 23 March. The examination took place at 29 India Street, and was attended by Barstow, two of the Commissioners, and Mr Campbell representing the Hamilton Trustees (to whom Roderick owed a mere £3,500). Roderick was accompanied by his agent, Mr Russell. The account of this meeting in the Sederunt Books provides an interesting and amusing spectacle of verbal swordplay between the Edinburgh solicitor and the former captain of dragoons!

38. The house in India Street, Edinburgh, where Roderick was eventually interrogated about his affairs by the Trustees on 23 March 1837.

Barstow began by asking Macneil to explain Harold Littledale's interest in the chemical works. Littledale had taken a lease of the works for three years, for an annual rent of £415. Two years of the lease had now expired said Roderick, but Littledale had yet to pay him a penny of the rent. Barstow then asked Macneil how much he still owed for freight charges on kelp he had bought from Uist. Roderick said he couldn't remember the exact figure but it was more than £200, possibly as much as £300, but certainly not as much as £400. It may be that this was a trick question from Barstow since figures were available to him showing the amount to be £226; if so, then Roderick's answer may have persuaded Barstow that he was, after all, dealing with an honest man.

It was time to press Macneil on more sensitive matters. Why, asked Barstow, had Macneil sent furniture and personal effects to Maceachern in Arisaig? Why, said Roderick, because his agent had told him that his Glasgow creditors were planning to seize all these items for themselves, and he, Roderick, was anxious that they should be available to his creditors at large. In that case, said Barstow, why did he not inform the Trustees and Charles Shaw of his actions and motives? Roderick said he had shipped the items off to Arisaig before he knew of either the Trustees' or Shaw's appointment. (this was clearly untrue). But, Barstow persisted, why then had he not told Shaw when he visited Barra? Well said Roderick, he hadn't told Shaw because Shaw hadn't asked him.

Barstow now turned to the poverty of the personal effects recorded at Barra House. Surely, said Barstow, a man like Macneil must have a set of silver plate? Roderick, perhaps choosing his words carefully, replied that at the time of sequestration he did not possess any silver plate and had not removed anything from Barra House since returning there last August. What about wine? said Barstow. There was a large sum owing to Bell Rennie. How much wine had Macneil purchased in the preceding year, and where was it now? Roderick said he really couldn't remember how much wine he had bought, but whatever it was it had all been drunk.

Getting nowhere on the whereabouts of personal effects, Barstow returned to Macneil's dealings with Michael Maceachern. Why had he shipped fifty-five head of cattle to him in October? Because he had sold them to Maceachern in June or July, said Roderick, but had allowed Maceachern to graze them at Eoligarry until he could arrange their shipment. But where had Macneil's bull gone? There were rumours it had been sent to Fassifern, where the Colonels in-laws lived. Roderick replied that he had sold the bull for £30 to Macneil of Canna last summer, and he thought that perhaps this bull might have been sent on to Fassifern. Had he not also sold cattle to Maclean of Glenforsland and Macmillan of Kilbride asked Barstow. Roderick said he had not sold them any cattle after last August. Barstow, probably despairing of wringing any admission of wrong-doing from Macneil, tried one more direct question to Macneil. 'Have you taken away, or not accounted for, any of your personal property or effects since sequestration?' 'No,' said Roderick, 'I have not.'

At this point the examination was concluded. It must have been clear to Barstow and his colleagues that Macneil was not being entirely honest with them, several of his answers being contrary to the known facts. But he was proving a resilient examinee. They told him he would have to come for a further interrogation in a fortnight's time. This duly took place on 6 April, but in the face of much the same questions as before, Roderick gave much the same answers. In particular he again denied ever having possession of a set of silver plate. A fortnight later on 19 April 1837 the ancestral estate of the Macneils of Barra was put up for sale with a reserve of £65,000, at the Coffee House at the Royal Exchange in Edinburgh, but there were no bidders. A month later on 23 May, at Barra House, Eoligarry, Macneil's personal effects (such as they had been able to lay hands on) and the livestock of the estate were auctioned off.

Macneil took himself off to Glasgow, and from there to meet with his wife in Ireland. It was definitely a time to avoid his acquaintances in London and Liverpool society. Word had inevitably got about not only concerning his bankruptcy but also the disappearance of his personal effects and rumours of dodgy or even illegal dealings in livestock. The social stigma that was beginning to attach to him is revealed in a letter by Alexander Hunter of London, in a letter to the Trustees written in June 1836. Regarding the rumours of illicit cattle dealing, he said that were they 'to remain uncontradicted Barra could never get a discharge and his character would be forever branded with infamy'. Noting that Macneil had denied possession of silver plate, Hunter wrote: 'I can swear to Barra having a very handsome service of plate,' adding (tongue in cheek?) 'which must have been stolen by someone.' He concluded that he hoped Macneil would be able to clear his name 'for the honour of a Highland chieftain'.

The matter of the silver plate weighed heavily on the Trustees' minds, and they wrote to Macneil again asking him about its whereabouts. He replied from Dublin and stated categorically: 'I was never owner of a considerable quantity of plate.' In their letter to him the Trustees had revealed the identity of the man who had probably been Shaw's secret informer when he had been in Barra in October 1836. According to his grieve, they wrote, he had possessed silver cutlery and fine linen which had been neither inventoried nor subsequently discovered. This man was presumably Thomas Parry, Macneil's last estate factor, to whom he allegedly owed £536 in unpaid wages. Parry would have had both the motive, and the information, to act as informer for Shaw. Roderick dismissed the allegations, saying that the man was a well known drunkard. 'Can I suppose that on the occasion he was admitted to my table he employed himself in counting the forks and spoons and examining the materials. What then could he know of quantity or quality?' But the questions about the silverware rumbled on. In October Macneil refused to answer further questions about it. But when the Trustees on 29 November prepared a list of fifty further questions to be put to Macneil the whereabouts of the silver plate was among them. Barstow noted bitterly that 'the transactions are involved in much mystery, contradiction and suspicion'.

Macneil simply ignored their further requests for answers but offered, through a go-between, to submit to further examination in Edinburgh if the Trustees would pay his expenses and give him 'protection' while he was there. The Trustees, had meanwhile been in touch with Macneil's military agents, trying to get their hands on his half-pay. The agents replied they were already receiving part of his pay to meet a prior debt. So the Trustees decided to approach the War Office to see if they would set aside moneys from Macneil's half-pay to cover his expenses at a further examination. They also decided to apply for a warrant to compel both Roderick and his wife to attend an interrogation. But nothing came of all this. In April 1838 Macneil sent a letter answering some of the questions put in the Trustees letter of November, but not surprisingly he made no concessions to his previous answers. By a mixture of prevarication, denial, obfuscation and silence, he had managed to grind down the Trustees' resolve to discover both the truth and the missing items. He now effectively disappears from view for three years, most probably living in deliberate exile and obscurity in Ireland, dependent perhaps on the goodwill and support of his wife's family.

The Trustees finally gave up pursuit of these matters as they sought to bring the whole sorry episode to a conclusion. The estate had already been put up for sale three times without attracting a single bidder. The estate for which Macneil claimed he had been offered £75,000 in August 1836 was now on the market at £60,000. Two more attempts in the autumn of 1838 saw the reserve fall to a mere £47,000 but still no buyer came forward. Finally on 6 March 1839, once more in the Coffee House of the Edinburgh Royal Exchange, offers were made. Bidding started at £36,000 and moved up to £42,050 before the sand in the half-hour glass ran out. The successful bidder was Mr Menzies, an Edinburgh solicitor. But he failed to come up with the cash, and the under-bidder, a Mr Warrington of Godstone in Surrey presented a cheque which bounced. And so the offer passed to Colonel John Gordon of Cluny, who had in fact being sizing up the estate since at least 1837 and perhaps even longer. There followed a prolonged wrangle over the price to be paid, the top two bids having proved fraudulent. Eventually Barra and its islands were sold to Gordon for £38,050 on 16 December 1839.

Ten years later, Gordon began his infamous evictions which in the space of three years saw perhaps 1,100 crofters, cottars and their

39. The Royal Exchange and the entrance to one of its coffee houses, where the Macneil estate was repeatedly put up for sale by auction before being eventually bought by Colonel John Gordon of Cluny.

families shipped off to either the central lowlands of Scotland or Quebec. Roderick Macneil has inevitably become associated with this event as the laird who lost Barra, although it was not he who sold it to Gordon of course, but Charles Murray Barstow and his Trustees. Roderick had been guilty of some extravagant personal expenditure but the bulk of his debts were either inherited from his father or the result of his desperate gamble on the chemical works. For a period of perhaps ten years (1826–36) he had tried to turn around the ruinous affairs of the estate to the best of his limited knowledge of farming and business. He had done so of course entirely for his own financial salvation, and he had become increasingly hard in his dealings with his kinsmen and tenants. One suspects that after he sailed away from Barra in March 1837 they never again entered his thoughts. Given his circumstances at that time, he certainly had other things to think about.

9

'This is a very unwholesome country': Roderick Takes the Queen's Rupee

By October 1836 Roderick Macneil, forty-first Chief of the Clan , found himself financially ruined and facing social disgrace. He had of course known it was coming for some time, and he had apparently already given some thought both to the immediate situation and to the future. We have seen how he had attempted to put much of his personal belongings, and some of his estate's livestock, beyond the reach of the Trustees and creditors, even before it was sequestered. He hid himself away in Barra where the Trustees could not easily reach him and then sent his wife to Ireland, probably to prepare the way for him to retreat there in May 1837.

Three months to the day after he went bankrupt, and apparently out-of-the-blue, Roderick was promoted to the army rank of Colonel. Although he was still not attached to a regiment and was on half-pay, this must have been a welcome boost both to his income and his morale. It will be remembered that the Trustees had already tried to get their hands on some of his army pay but had been rebuffed by the War Office. One wonders whether Roderick had a friend at the War Office who looked after his interests in this difficult time. The Commander-in-Chief at this time, Sir Rowland Hill, had fought in the same battles as Roderick – at Vimiero and Corunna, and later at Waterloo – but it is unlikely that he had ever noticed this lowly ensign and captain. If Roderick had a friend in the War Office it must have been someone of more modest rank on the C-in-C's staff.

In any event, whether at Roderick's promptings or by sheer coincidence, his promotion at this time was the first step towards him once again taking up his career in the British army. However, in the immediate aftermath of the bankruptcy and his devious handling of his assets, rumours and accounts of which had clearly reached London, he could not expect an early return to a regiment. He would have to bide his time and he would also have to consider taking an overseas posting. Meanwhile, it was best to keep a low profile, and that is what he managed to do. Between May 1837 and July 1841 his whereabouts are unknown. He was 'last heard of' in Dublin, his wife having preceded him to Ireland. A retreat to Ireland was an obvious and sensible option for the now impoverished Chief. His wife's brother, Charles Brownlow of Lurgan, Armagh, had married Macneil's sister Jane in 1828, so the family bond was doubly strong. The Brownlows were a wealthy family and were well able to take care of Roderick and Isabella while affairs were sorted and social wounds healed.

Roderick reappears in the records in July 1841 when he became regimental Lieutenant Colonel of the 91st Argyllshire Regiment of Foot. He obtained this position by exchanging with Lieutenant Colonel Burne who wanted to go on half-pay for medical reasons. But Roderick seems to have been reluctant to take up his new command. The regimental muster rolls record him as 'not joined' and worse, on several occasions, 'absent without leave'! Regimental history remembers him as having refused to take command of the regiment unless and until it was allowed to resume wearing the kilt. At no time previously in his military or his civilian life had Roderick played the role of the proud Scotsman. Only one of his previous seven regiments had been Scottish, and he had spent most of his adult life in England until the dire position of his estate forced him to return to Barra. Furthermore, he must have known that his predecessor, Lieutenant Colonel Burne, had sought permission for the 91st to wear the kilt and had been refused. His firm stand on the 91st's right to wear the kilt was almost certainly a matter of neither pride nor principle but a convenient excuse to delay taking up his command. The reason for that may have been because the 91st were serving abroad and their two battalions were split between South Africa and providing a garrison for the bleak and very remote island of St Helena. The thought of being posted there may have been enough to make Roderick drag his feet. But pressure mounted on him, and in January he was given unequivocal orders to join his regiment at the Cape of Good Hope without delay. He submitted a petition to take his oath, but somehow still managed to put off the evil day of embarkation.

Nine months after he had been appointed to the 91st, just when it seemed he could no longer delay actually joining his regiment, he managed to exchange with Lieutenant Colonel Lindsey of the 78th Highlanders. So perhaps he really was committed to commanding a Scottish regiment after all? Perhaps, but it seems more likely that the 78th not only provided an escape route from the possibility of ending up on St Helena but also opened up possibilities for re-building his modest fortune. Macneil took up his appointment with the 78th on 15 April 1842. Six days later he and his regiment set sail for India! Macneil must have known that the regiment was about to leave for India when he took up the command. Roderick clearly made a conscious choice between serving in South Africa or serving in India.

Although officers who served in India were still treated as somewhat inferior creatures to those who didn't, it was widely recognized that

40. The 78th Highlanders in 1846. Roderick was their Lieutenant Colonel from 1842 to 1855, but spent much of this time on staff duties elsewhere in India.

India provided exceptional opportunities to make money and gain advancement. As well as receiving additional pay for serving in India there was sufficient military action to yield prize money and loot. There were also better opportunities to be promoted to divisional commands, with further additions to your salary. At the same time houses, food, servants and horses were all very cheap to acquire, so that you and your family could live in considerable luxury for a fraction of what it cost to live in modest style in London.

So it was probably with some relief and some anticipation that Lieutenant Colonel Roderick Macneil, Mrs Macneil, and Miss Caroline Macneil went aboard the three-masted barque the *Bussorah Merchant* at Gravesend. There were four other officers and 174 men of the regiment, plus forty camp followers, on board the ship when she left port. The rest of the regiment were embarked on five other ships, sent to India to help replace the troops lost in the debacle of the retreat from Kabul in the 1st Afghan War the year before. The *Bussorah Merchant* had been used for a time to transport convicts

41. The *Bussorah Merchant*, the three-masted barque and former convict transport on which Macneil, his wife and daughter sailed for India in 1842.

to Australia before being converted to carry emigrants to the same destination, so that even for officers it could provide only modest comforts. The voyage to India would be a long, tedious, and at times uncomfortable one. It was broken only at Cape Town where, while the ship replenished supplies, Macneil and his family, along with other officers, were able to go ashore for a few days.

Eventually, after fourteen weeks at sea, the *Bussorah Merchant* sailed into the harbour at Bombay on 31 July. Bombay was a cosmopolitan city crammed with sailors and merchants from all parts of Europe, Africa and Asia. 'On all sides are seen Persian dyers, Bannian shop-keepers, Chinese with long tails, Arab horse-dealers, Abyssinian youths, Armenian priests with flowing robes and beards, Jews in long tunics and mantles.' The Macneils spent about a week in Bombay, recovering from the voyage and absorbing the sights and sounds of this busy port, no doubt joining the throngs of Europeans who each evening strolled by the waterfront along the open spaces of the Esplanade.

Then it was time to move on to Poona, 100 miles south-east of Bombay. Macneil arrived there on 11 August. Poona had been the capital of the powerful Marathas in the eighteenth century but by 1840 it was where the Bombay army had its headquarters. In 1841 Sir Charles Napier, shortly to become known as the conqueror of Sind, had taken up command of the forces there. The 78th took up garrison duties in the two cantonments, one east of the city and the other nearby at Kirkee. Situated 2,000 feet above sea level, Poona was cooler than Bombay and somewhat healthier, though set in a bare and almost treeless landscape. One of Roderick's men in the 78th Highlanders wrote home from Poona on Christmas Day that year with the cheerful news that 'this is a very unwholesome country... there is many that is caught of very sudden for they are taken ill in a minute and in two or three hours they are called into eternity. We have lost a good many men since we came here and (are) always losing more'.

The regiment comprised two battalions, each notionally of 980 men, one commanded by Lieutenant Colonel Douglas and the other

42. A mid-nineteenth century view of Poona, where Roderick was stationed, commanding a battalion of the 78th Highlanders between 1842 and 1848.

by Macneil, each of whom was assisted by two majors. The 78th spent the winter of 1842 at Poona, during which time one is tempted to believe that Roderick Macneil learned the secrets of the Indian rope-trick! Although he was to serve in India for another twelve years, throughout this period he is almost invisible, glimpsed only briefly at infrequent intervals. Only the bare outlines of his service in India can be traced in the records.

In November and December 1842, he is noted as serving 'on Staff employ' at Poona. As we shall see, this episode may have whetted his taste for Staff duties. In June 1843 his daughter Caroline married John Haliburton, a Lieutenant in her father's regiment. According to military records, at this time Macneil was commanding the Poona Brigade, a command he held throughout 1843 and 1844. This command must explain why, when the 78th moved to Karachi at the end of 1843, it was under the command not of Lieutenant Colonel Macneil (nor indeed of Lieutenant Colonel Douglas – who was on 'special duties') – but a mere major. But Macneil, commanding the brigade of which the 78th was a part, moved with them. By now Napier had secured the Sind and was preparing to move against the northern tribes who posed a threat to British control of the region. The 78th were among the regiments who were to take part in this action and they marched from Karachi to Sukhur, avoiding the worst of the suffocating heat by marching at night and in the early hours of daylight. They nevertheless fell prey to fever or cholera, and between September 1844 and April 1845 they lost 535 officers and men and 202 camp followers. It was a devastating experience, made all the worse by malicious rumours which initially ascribed the 78th's inability to fight to intemperance! For Roderick it must have been a case of *deja vu* as he recalled the fever-led catastrophe of the Walcheren expedition thirty years before.

What remained of the 78th, having played no part in Napier's successful campaign, was evacuated from Sukhur by boat to Hyderabad in late December, and then by steamer in February and March 1845 to Bombay. Many of the survivors were sent back to Britain, too weak to be of any further use. The regiment returned to Poona in April to lick its wounds and to start recruiting replacements wherever it could find them. When Roderick arrived home in Poona, he found he had become a grandfather. With Lieutenant Haliburton on campaign with the 78th, his daughter had moved in with Mrs Macneil and had given birth on 11 December to a baby girl, Isabella Ellen. This was to be his only grandchild.

Although Roderick's regiment had played no active part in the Sind campaigns, Roderick was now given command not only of a brigade but of a division. Captain Ramsay of the 14th Light Dragoons, who was ADC to the Governor of Bombay from 1845, recalled Roderick in his memoirs: 'The division was commanded by a very fine old soldier, Roderick Macneil, 78th Highlanders, who had formerly been in the Life Guards.' Divisional command brought with it a salary of £4,000 per annum. Further promotion followed in 1846 when he was raised, brevet, to the army rank of Major General, retaining his regimental rank and still commanding a division of the Bombay army. Promotion by brevet would normally follow some distinguished performance in the field but unless Roderick had been active with the remainder of his brigade in Sind, there would have been no opportunity since the return to Poona to demonstrate his military skills or courage.

Nevertheless, the army seemed pleased with Roderick Macneil. In 1848 he was not only given a Distinguished Service Award (with a cash sum of £100) but more importantly he was appointed to command the centre division of the Madras army. The Madras army totalled about 70,000 men, of whom 85 per cent were native troops. Seven British infantry regiments and the 15th Hussars formed the core of the force. The centre division, with something like 20,000 men, was the biggest force that Roderick had ever commanded. Madras, however, was generally regarded as the most peaceful of the three 'presidencies' in India and there was little for the troops to do most of the time. There were minor native uprisings, which were successfully put down, and the British took stern measures to stamp out the practice of *meriah* or human sacrifice. But otherwise the British troops and their officers led quiet lives.

Madras itself was much less cosmopolitan than Bombay and had a healthier climate. The British residents there lived in some luxury with large houses fronted by porticoes and set in spacious compounds. Major General Macneil no doubt acquired a house befitting his rank, and on his divisional salary he could afford to staff it generously with servants and entertain the great and the good. At such events Mrs Macneil may have provided some of the entertainment, for according to Captain Ramsay she was 'an extremely clever woman, at the same time very eccentric'. He described an incident when the Macneils were in Poona. 'All the officers of our regiment, including my Colonel, William Havelock, who was a great advocate of the water-cure came up to pay their respects to her. She asked them severally to dinner, with the exception of Colonel Havelock, whom she addressed thus: 'It is no use asking you to dinner Colonel Havelock, as you do not like champagne; but if you will come and take a cold bath with me some morning, I shall be delighted to see you.' Isabella Macneil was, perhaps, a lady of some spirit.

Roderick's three-year appointment to command the Centre Division drew to a close early in 1851, but just as he was due to return to

43. A European house at Madras *c.*1840. As a Major General commanding a division of the Madras army Roderick was able to live in some style in Madras in a spacious house surrounded and pampered by a large staff of servants.

the 78th at Bombay it was announced that he had been seconded for six months to the General Staff in Madras, replacing Major General Aitchison. Roderick must have been pleased since a staff appointment carried higher emoluments and greater prestige than regimental duties. Furthermore, the 78th's two wings were now taking it in turn to garrison Britain's latest acquisition in the region – the hot and arid port at Aden. Neither Roderick nor his wife would have been keen to swap the pleasures of Madras for the rigours on Aden.

Had he any doubts about the wisdom of avoiding Aden, Macneil had the opportunity in the autumn of 1851 to see for himself what a god-forsaken hole it was. It appears that he and Mrs Macneil visited Egypt at this time, presumably as tourists during a spell of leave. They are recorded leaving Suez on the steamer *Oriental* on 9 October, calling at Aden on the 15th, and arriving back at Bombay on the 28th. It would be interesting to know if Macneil went ashore in Aden, to visit the men of his regiment. At the time, the battalion of the 78th in garrison at Aden was that which, had he not been on duties in Madras, Macneil would have been commanding. He may have felt it prudent to keep a low profile.

116

But he was now due, on the day he arrived in Bombay, to re-join his regiment, and his sight of Aden may have spurred him on, if he needed encouragement, to avoid duty in the field and in particular in Aden. Miraculously, he was greeted in Bombay with the news that as from 28 October he was to serve a further twelve months on the General Staff of the Madras Centre Division. So he and Mrs Macneil returned to the pleasures of life in Madras. How this appointment came about we do not know, but again one suspects it was not mere chance but that Macneil had managed to cultivate friends in the right places during his three years in the presidency. The Commander in Chief of the Madras Army at this time was Sir William Sewell who as a young man, two years older than Roderick, had fought with Sir John Moore's forces and taken part in the retreat to Corunna. It is unlikely that they ever met during those horrendous weeks in the Cantabrian Mountains, but the bond which Corunna veterans felt may at least have found Sewell well-disposed to any recommendation for Macneil's appointment which came before him. Roderick made the best of his opportunity and his appointment was continued from October 1851 through to the end of 1854. We know nothing of his activities in this period but they would have been largely routine administration. Fortune, or his superiors, continued to smile on him, however, and in June 1854 he was raised brevet to the army rank of Lieutenant General.

There are two remaining mysteries concerning Macneil's service in India. One is a trifling matter but intriguing. On 19 February 1854, the wife of Captain John Alexander Campbell of the 7th Regiment of Madras Light Infantry gave birth to the couple's fourth child. The three previous children had been soberly christened Alexander, Frederick and Constance. But when the new son was christened a week later, he was named Roderick Macneil Alexander Campbell. This can hardly be other than a doffing of the cap to our Lieutenant General, but why? Had Macneil done Captain Alexander a favour, or was Alexander perhaps seconded to work for him?

The other matter is potentially more significant, but also more baffling. When Macneil wrote his will in 1859 he mentioned among

44. Government House at Madras which Roderick must have got to know well during the seven years he served in the Madras presidency.

the bequests 'my freehold house at Calcutta'. We have no record that Macneil ever visited Calcutta, let alone took up residence there. It is difficult to see when, during his thirteen years in India, he could have spent any time in the city. It was far removed from both Bombay and Madras, and it was not the sort of place where high-ranking officers went to avoid the heat in the summer months! The only period when he could have spent time in Calcutta was between the end of his service on General Staff in Madras (November 1854) and his return to England (in March 1855). Why he should go to Calcutta in this period is open to speculation. It may have been simply to see the capital of British India before he returned to Britain, or perhaps he had some official duties that took him there. But this would hardly explain the purchase of a house. That would surely imply that he expected to take up residence in Calcutta. Was he expecting a posting to Staff duties at Army HQ there?

If he did, then it never materialized. On 28 February 1855 he and Mrs Macneil boarded the P&O steamship *Hindostan* at Madras, en route for Suez. He was due for furlough at this time and it is possible that he intended to return to India. It may be that he purchased a house in Calcutta with that intention in mind. But events overtook him, and he never returned to the sub-continent. He left behind him his only daughter and grand-daughter, and of course his regiment. Two years later soldiers of the 78th won eight Victoria Crosses for their exploits in the Indian Mutiny, seven of them in the relief and defence of Lucknow. Some officers might have thought it rotten luck to have so narrowly missed the chance to win lasting fame and honours. But I doubt that Roderick, by then in his sixty-seventh year, and having spent the last three years in India on Staff duties, entertained such thoughts. India had served him well. Opportunities for prize-money had been few, but a good salary and additional emoluments must have enabled him to accumulate some capital. Twenty years on, his bankruptcy and devious dealings with the Trustees were hopefully forgotten. As the *Hindostan* slipped anchor at Madras, General and Mrs Macneil could look forward with some confidence to returning to England.

A Footnote

While Roderick was serving in Poona in 1845, a baby girl was born to Mr and Mrs Robert Pringle in Madras. Pringle had arrived in India to work in the Madras Civil Service in 1836. In September 1844 he married Hester McNeill, one of the Gigha McNeills and possibly a distant relative of the General. Their daughter was christened Emily Eliza. Twenty years later, when she was just twenty, she married John Gordon, now the owner of the estate of Barra following the death of his father, Colonel Gordon of Cluny. When her husband died in 1878, Emily Gordon (née Pringle) became the owner of General Macneil's former estate. She subsequently married Lord Cathcart and became Lady Gordon Cathcart. She held the estate of Barra for fifty-four years until her death in 1932 – almost four times as long as the estate was in the General's hands! The family left Madras in 1847, just a year before the General took up his command there.

10

'The gallant General':
Roderick's Return

The first leg of the journey home certainly promised to be more relaxed and pleasant than the journey out thirteen years previously. The *Hindostan* was a steamship driven by paddles, built to order for the Peninsular and Oriental Steam Navigation Company, specifically to ply between Calcutta and Suez. It had cost the P&O over £60,000 and at 2,000 tons was the biggest ship in their new fleet. With its three tall masts and two upright white funnels it was an impressive sight. By contemporary standards it was luxurious too with spacious fitted cabins, the better ones with their own hot and cold baths or showers. One imagines the General would have acquired one of the three best double cabins on the upper deck, where Isabella could also socialize in the lady's drawing room. In the dining room at the stern of the upper deck sumptuous meals were served.

When the ship called at Ceylon there may have been opportunity for a few hours ashore, but since the ship earned its keep partly by carrying mails there were no unnecessary delays. After Ceylon there was only one further call – at Aden, of which the Macneils had probably seen all they wanted on their visit to Egypt in 1851. After three and a half weeks at sea, the *Hindostan* docked at Suez. Suez was a hive of activity as both an important communications hub and a coaling station, but it was not a particularly healthy or pleasant place to be. As soon as possible the Macneils would have boarded one of the six-seater horse-drawn omnibuses which would take them across sixty miles of desert to Cairo and the Nile – the Suez Canal still being fourteen years in the future!

The cross-desert journey took a day and a half, of which twelve hours were spent in resting and changing the horses and the

45. The P&O steamship *Hindostan* on which Roderick and Mrs Macneil sailed from Madras to Aden in 1855. Its best cabins offered a choice of hot and cold baths and showers.

46. The busy port of Suez at the time Roderick and his wife arrived there in 1855 on the way home to England.

passengers taking the chance to stretch their legs and take refreshment at one of the 'stations' provided for them. After the comfort of the *Hindostan* this journey must have been, at the very least, tedious and uncomfortable. One passenger who took this route a year after the Macneils was less than enthusiastic about it. It 'could hardly be called enjoyable, even when the tedium was relieved by drinking

47. A way station on the overland route from Suez to the Nile, over which Macneil and his wife travelled in one of the six-seater horse-drawn omnibuses seen in this contemporary painting.

innumerable cups of coffee at the various stations where the horses were changed. It was followed by unrefreshing sleep, too frequently disturbed by the stab of the mosquito or the furious assaults of all-pervading and insatiate fleas'. When they reached Cairo, the Macneils and other passengers going to Alexandria transferred onto one of the P&O's river steamers for the journey up the Nile to Atfeh. Here, they again had to disembark and board a barge pulled by a steam tug which took them at a gentle pace the remaining fifty miles by canal to Alexandria.

At Alexandria, after only a brief delay, the Macneils boarded a steam packet for England. All being well, the journey would take twelve or thirteen days. It appears that Isabella had been ill for about a week by this time, so that the journey from Suez to Alexandria must have been particularly debilitating for her. The journey through the Mediterranean would perhaps give her a chance to recuperate but it was March and taking the air on deck could be a chilly business. Once they passed the Straits of Gibraltar cold winds and rougher

48. The Dolphin Hotel, Southampton, where Isabella Macneil died of 'bronchitis' only a few days after returning from India in April 1855.

seas were likely, so she was probably confined to her cabin until the ship reached Southampton.

They arrived there in the middle of April. Any plans to move on to London were postponed since Isabella's condition had worsened. Instead they booked into the Dolphin Hotel on Southampton High Street, where Jane Austen had attended the winter balls some fifty years earlier. The doctor diagnosed Isabella's illness as bronchitis, but was unable to treat it. On 21 April, with Roderick at her bedside, Isabella died. She was sixty-eight. Roderick purchased a plot in what is now known as Southampton Old Cemetery, and Isabella was buried there in a fine mausoleum built of Aberdeen granite. On its west face was carved a coat of arms, flanked and supported by lions, which incorporated the arms of the Macneils of Barra and another unidentified coat of arms. On the north face Roderick had the following inscription carved:

Sacred to the memory of Isabella Caroline, the affectionate devoted and much loved wife of Lieut General Roderick

Macneil of that Ilk and Barra Invernesshire.
The beloved and exemplary daughter of the late Charles
Brownlow of Lurgan County of Armagh Esq and sister of the
late Lord Lurgan.
Died at Southampton on the 21st April 1855, to the deep
grief of her husband, much lamented by her family and
friends

We have no letters or memoirs of Roderick's to tell us how much
he grieved for his wife, and the inscription on the tomb follows
a formula widely found on contemporary gravestones. Isabella
had been a loyal wife to Macneil for almost forty years, standing
alongside him and aiding and abetting him during his financial
disgrace in the mid 1830s, and spending thirteen years with him on
service in India. One or two later clues suggest that Roderick was in
fact very much attached to Isabella.

After Isabella's funeral he returned to London, and found himself
an apartment on Bond Street. At some time during his journey back

49. The coat of arms carved on the tomb of Isabella Macneil in Southampton
Old Cemetery.

from India he would have been informed that he had been given a new appointment as Colonel of the 8th King's Regiment of Foot. Its previous Colonel, Lieutenant General Duffy, had died on 18 March when the *Hindostan* was somewhere between Ceylon and Aden. Roderick's appointment to replace him appeared in the London Gazette on 6 April, when the Macneils were somewhere *en route* between Alexandria and Southampton, so the news may have awaited him when he landed. At that time, Isabella's illness must have been foremost in his mind but now, unexpectedly alone in London, he could give some thought to his new command.

Colonels of regiments were not, of course, expected to undertake active service of any sort, they were essentially ceremonial positions. But they were responsible for the provision of their regiment's uniform and received a government grant to purchase it. Since the grant could be claimed for the notional, rather than the actual, strength of a unit, it was possible to make a profit from uniform purchases, but by the mid-nineteenth century it was rarely done. The Colonel might attend important functions of the regiment, but since the 8th King's were serving in India Roderick would have had no opportunity to do so, even if he wished to. However, the Colonelcy of the 8th King's Regiment of Foot gave Roderick a new status among his acquaintances and fellow members of the United Services Club.

The USC had been founded in 1815, originally for officers who had served in the Napoleonic Wars, of which Roderick Macneil of course was one. It was said to be the Duke of Wellington's favourite club and had many famous officers, as well as members of the royal family, among its members. It had moved into its prestigious new home in Pall Mall, designed by John Nash, in 1828, and it was less than a quarter of a mile from the General's apartment on Bond Street. In the months following Isabella's death it may well have provided an important social haven for him, where he could meet old acquaintances and discuss the events of the day. Apart from any reputation he had earned himself, he may also have benefited by his relationship to Colonel John Cameron, who led a distinguished military career and received various honours from King George, culminating in the Order of the Bath. Cameron was Roderick's maternal uncle. He had died at Quatre Bras in 1815, but his relationship to Roderick was certainly remembered by Lieutenant General William Brereton when a memoir on Colonel Cameron was published in 1858. Roderick received a rather gushing letter from Brereton, who had fought alongside Cameron at Salamanca and had found the memoir of 'your noble and truly heroic uncle' very moving. 'I have indeed been gratified in reading this simple narrative and though you will hardly believe me I can assure you that at parts of it I have been deeply affected.'

When the Indian Mutiny broke out in 1857 as a senior officer with thirteen years experience in India, and as the Colonel of one of the regiments involved in putting down the insurrection Roderick no doubt had the opportunity to share his views and experiences with his fellow members at the Club. The 8th King's were heavily involved

50. The United Services Club in Pall Mall, London, where Roderick found the company of fellow veterans in the early days of his return to England.

in the siege and capture of Delhi, during which they suffered severe losses, and the relief of Agra and Cawnpore. At Lucknow they fought alongside Roderick's previous regiment, the 78th Highlanders. Roderick presumably basked in a certain amount of reflected glory as the news of their victories filtered back to London.

Seemingly out of the blue, in 1858 the General re-married! On 14 October at St George's Church in Hanover Square, Roderick married Eliza Middleton, the widow of Charles Middleton, who had died in London in 1844. They shared at least two common interests – India and the army. Eliza was the daughter of George Carpenter who had served for decades in the Bengal army, rising to the rank of Brigadier General. She was the youngest of Carpenter's four children and was born in India in 1811. Her older sisters were probably born there too, and both married members of the East India Company civil service. Mary's husband, Stewart Paxton, seems to have dabbled in the arms trade as well! Mary and Jane produced eight children between them, but child-bearing and the climate took its toll and both died in India in early middle age in the 1830s. Eliza's brother, George, followed his father into the army and by 1834 had risen to captain in His Majesty's 41st Regiment of Foot. Eliza also had two step-sisters, from her mother Hester's first marriage, and these too had married soldiers, so the Carpenters were a very military family!

As for Eliza's first husband, he had served in the Indian civil service in Bengal. He was twenty years older than Eliza and the two of them returned to England about the same time that Roderick sailed for India. They set up home in Marylebone but in January 1844 Charles Middleton died at the age of fifty-three, and Eliza found herself a widow. She initially moved in with her father and mother in Great Cumberland Place, her father now well into his eighties, having returned to England in 1834. The Brigadier General died early in 1855, just before Roderick returned from India.

Just how Roderick and Eliza met is a mystery, but it is unlikely it had much to do with India. Roderick can never have met Eliza or her parents in India; they were never there at the same time. It is

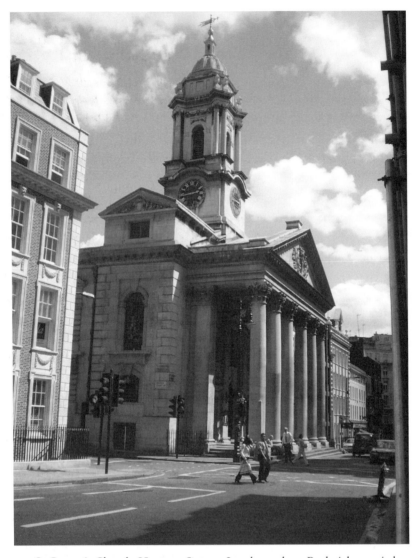

51. St George's Church, Hanover Square, London, where Roderick married Eliza Middleton on 14 October 1858.

very unlikely they met in England between 1834 and 1842, when Roderick was keeping a very low profile and probably spent most of this time in Scotland and Ireland. It is just possible that they became acquainted in Southampton at the time of Isabella's illness and death. The Middleton family lived at Midanbury, Southampton, and both of Eliza's brothers-in-law had near relations in the area. By chance, we know that Eliza kept in touch with at least one of these families. On census day in 1861, who should be staying overnight with Eliza and Roderick but Eliza's niece, Annie Hessie Paxton, now a widow, and her two sons George and Harry. Annie's grandmother, Dame Ann Paxton, lived at Upton Gray, between Basingstoke and Southampton. So Eliza could have been visiting relatives in or around Southampton in April 1855 – but it must remain a remote possibility that she was, and that she met the Macneils in that brief period. Otherwise we must assume that Eliza and Roderick met at some social event or other in London some time after Brigadier General Carpenter's death.

Carpenter was a wealthy man, his will (written in 1834) leaving almost 700,000 Rupees (about £70,000) in bonds as well as annuities of £2,000 a year to Hester and a lump sum of £1,000 to Eliza. What Charles Middleton left Eliza when he died in 1844 we do not know,

52. Hyde Park Gardens, the impressive terrace overlooking Hyde Park where Roderick and Eliza settled after their marriage.

but the Middletons too were a wealthy family and Eliza was probably well provided for. After her father's death she moved into a fine town house overlooking Hyde Park, at 35 Hyde Park Gardens, and it was here that she was living when she married Roderick. Not surprisingly he moved out of his widower's apartment on Bond Street and into Eliza's house. Here, he and Eliza could live in some style. The census of 1861 records their household as including a cook, a lady's maid, a housemaid, a kitchen maid, a footman and a butler.

The extent to which they played a part in London society is unknown. Roderick still presumably frequented the United Services Club which provided him with a ready-made group of friends and companions. Eliza having lived in London for almost twenty years had presumably built up a circle of acquaintances. Whether Roderick's bankruptcy and his dubious dealings in its aftermath were still remembered at all in London circles we do not know, but it may be that at least 'the establishment' had not forgotten the affair. Unlike the vast majority of other Generals and Colonels of Regiments, Roderick was never appointed either a Companion of the Bath or a Knight Commander of the Bath.

He must have been aware of this slight. The Lieutenant General he replaced as Colonel of the 8th King's Regiment of Foot had been a CB, and so had Lieutenant General Sir William Chalmers whose death on 3 July 1860 opened the way for Roderick to return to the 78th Highlanders as their Colonel. The regiment had returned to Britain from their triumphs in India in February, initially to Fort George near Inverness, and shortly after to Edinburgh. Here in March and April they had been entertained to two lavish banquets. On 9 August, a month after Roderick had become their Colonel, they were paraded for inspection by His Royal Highness the Duke of Cambridge (C-in-C) who pronounced them 'a noble regiment and admirably drilled'. At the same occasion they were presented with the medals they had won in India by Lady Havelock (widow of Sir Henry Havelock who had served with distinction in India while Macneil was there). It was the sort of occasion when one might expect the Colonel of the Regiment to be in attendance to share in

53. General Macneil, as Colonel of the 78th Highlanders, *c.*1860. A copy of a portrait by an unknown artist, the whereabouts of which is presently unknown.

his regiment's glory. But none of the accounts of this event mention the presence of General Macneil. Was he indisposed or disinterested, or was he perhaps still anxious to avoid returning to Edinburgh for other reasons?

He was proud enough of his Colonelcy of the 78th Highlanders to have his portrait painted in his full uniform, and the surviving photographic copy of this provides us with our only image of General Roderick Macneil. Alexander Carmichael later wrote 'that so symmetrical in person was General Macneil that no eye looked on him without looking at him again'. He is certainly an imposing figure with a fine bushy beard, a generous moustache and curling sidelocks. Over his short jacket with two deep pockets he wears a full plaid fixed on his left shoulder with a plaid brooch. From his belt, a dirk hangs over his kilt of Mackenzie of Seaforth tartan. His right hand is on his hip, and grasping his feathered bonnet, while his left is at his side gripping his sword. He is unsmiling and his eyes are narrowed, a severe and somewhat forbidding figure.

How much interest he took in his regiment is unknown. In early summer 1861 they were moved to Aldershot, and a year later to Shorncliffe, where Roderick had undergone his initial training as an ensign in the 52nd Light Infantry more than fifty years before. It would have been a relatively short journey to either camp to see his Regiment but whether he ever made the effort we do not know. In December 1862 he reached the peak of his military career, being promoted to full General. In May 1863 the 78th were moved the short distance from Shorncliffe to Dover, still well within travelling distance of their Colonel. On 17 October the first issue of prize money from the relief of Lucknow was issued to the men of the 78th. Five days later they mourned the death of their Colonel.

Roderick died, unexpectedly, at his home in Hyde Park Gardens on the morning of 22 October 1863. A brief account in a Southampton newspaper recorded the circumstances: 'The gallant General, who

54. Roderick and Isabella's mausoleum in Southampton Old Cemetery.

rose apparently in his usual good health on Thursday morning, retired to his dressing room for the purpose of shaving, and on the return of his valet and butler was found dead.'

If one believes his census return of 1861 he was sixty-eight when he died, but the cemetery records give his age as seventy-two and that seems to accord better with his entry into the army in March 1808. In his will Roderick left a £3,000 annuity for his only grandchild – Isabella Ellen Haliburton to whom he also bequeathed his morocco writing case and the oak box containing the jewellery of 'my late dear wife Isabella Caroline Macneil'. His daughter, Caroline, received only 'the dressing case which belonged to her late dear mother'. She was presumably well provided for by her husband, John Haliburton. Roderick left everything else to Eliza, including his house in Calcutta. Eliza, in a generous gesture and perhaps in accordance with his expressed wish, arranged for him to be buried alongside Isabella in the mausoleum in Southampton Old Cemetery. He was laid to rest on Thursday 29 October 1863.

11

'He was noble in character': Roderick in Retrospect

Looking back over the life of Roderick Macneil, forty-first Chief of the Clan Macneil, one can see that it reflects the changing fortunes and circumstances not only of the highland chiefs and their clans, but of the Scottish people as a whole in the period between 1745 and 1860. This is hardly surprising, for despite his chiefly status, and his army rank, he was just as much a pawn on the chessboard of social, economic and political change in this period as were his clansmen, tenants and foot soldiers.

The die was cast some thirty years before Roderick was born, when his grandfather having taken a commission in the army, laid down his life for King George at Quebec. As a result, his son and heir, not yet ten years old, was brought up by his uncle, a Presbyterian minister. The conversion of the Macneils from Catholicism was therefore more than a matter of political necessity and convenience, it became a conviction and a firm commitment to the Protestant faith. Given that 90 per cent of the population of Barra at this time were fiercely Catholic, this was bound to weaken the traditional relationship between the chief and his kinsmen. Perceived or real religious persecution was a more powerful motive in the emigrations of 1770, 1790, 1802, 1817 and 1821 than economic necessity. At the same time, Roderick's father set out to 'improve' his estate in line with the agricultural thinking of the time, touring the Low Countries to see how land was drained and cattle raised, and buying high quality livestock for his farm. The development of the 'home farm' at Eoligarry, with the enforced eviction of some tenants, erected a further barrier between him and his people. Further, the building of Barra House provided a stark contrast between the lifestyle of the chief and his clansmen, only emphasized by the way in which Roderick and his wife were portrayed by Raeburn. It was not so much Roderick the Gentle as Roderick the Gentleman Farmer.

Although we believe the General lived most of his early years on Barra, he was brought up by a father committed to Protestant gentility. His decision, at the age of sixteen, to join the army, or failing that take up some sort of business career, is hardly surprising. His father was by now a frequent visitor to Liverpool where he mixed with a circle of English businessmen, while his grandfather, father and maternal uncle had all served in the British army. The patronage of his father's old friend, Sir John Moore, enabled him to very quickly secure an ensignship in one of the elite Light Infantry regiments and held the prospect of rapid advancement.

In the space of seven years, Roderick experienced just about all the horrors that nineteenth-century warfare could offer. He was barely seventeen when he was embroiled in the desperate rearguard action covering the retreat to Corunna, during which he saw regular soldiers behaving like animals, and thousands of men, women and children dying of exposure and starvation. Within a year, he witnessed the decimation of his battalion by the rampant 'fever' (typhoid, cholera?) which swept through the British troops on the Walcheren expedition, killing fit, healthy young men in the space of hours and turning others into broken invalids for the rest of their lives. At the age of twenty three he was an eye-witness of the slaughter that was Waterloo, when men were blown apart by cannons, hacked to death by cavalry, or stabbed or shot by the massed ranks of infantry. Any young man who had been through these experiences might become hardened and insensitive to suffering and have a different idea of hardship and deprivation to the people back home.

The experiences did not, however, discourage Roderick from pursuing a career in the army and we know his father spent money he did not have to buy him promotions, eventually into the prestigious Life Guards. He also presumably funded Roderick's travels on the continent, and he was clearly delighted when Roderick married Isabella Brownlow, with a £6,000 dowry, and 'a prospect of more'.

During the years between entering the army and his father's death, a period of fourteen years, Roderick spent hardly any time at all in Scotland, let alone on Barra. He had become a stranger to his people and even, one suspects, to his father and his siblings. As his father was now living in Liverpool, Barra was run by factors and tacksmen and the chief became an increasingly distant figure.

When his father died, Roderick was initially faced with a long and debilitating struggle to regain control of the estate from the trustees. He was also saddled with a mountain of debts. When he finally regained control of the estate he tried to manage it from a remote distance, partly through his factors and partly by relying on the good offices of the parish priest. He revealed little understanding of the problems facing highland estates at this time, at first doing little more than tinkering with the way the estate was managed and trying to coerce his tenants into working harder and paying their rents promptly. Neither the priest nor his first factors proved reliable.

With the appointment of Alexander Stewart as factor, the attempts to put the estate on a sound financial footing were given a firm push in the direction of a classic 'improvement' package. Crofters were to be taken off the best land and relocated to more remote and barren areas where they would have to rely on fishing for the greater part of their livelihood. A village devoted to a fishing community was also to be built at Castlebay. The emptied crofts were to be turned into small farms for livestock and rented out to tenants from the mainland. Although the evictions began, it is not clear that Roderick was ever really committed to Stewart's programme. He certainly met fierce resistance from the crofters, who among other things threatened emigration, and in 1826 he lost more than 200 of them to Cape Breton.

Although he partly replaced them, as he had threatened to do, with Protestants from other parts of the highlands and islands, it may have been this emigration which convinced him that his improvement programme would fail. He now embarked on a huge gamble, taking on over the next seven years a series of large loans to finance his 'chemical works'. His plans to re-process kelp to produce a higher quality product were on a quite different scale to experiments in producing better kelp that were taking place on Uist. The whole enterprise, including the continued production of made kelp around the shores of Barra, must have employed several hundred workers, dozens of whom worked in the chemical factory at Northbay. Macneil brought the industrial revolution to Barra. His investment in the chemical works can be viewed as bold, desperate, or reckless. Indeed it may have been all three, but it was quite certainly a genuine attempt to turn around the financial situation of the estate.

When the gamble failed in 1836 Roderick faced a prolonged and painful battle-of-wits with the trustees and creditors as he sought to hold on to whatever assets he could hide away. He put as much distance between them and himself as he could by residing in Barra. He probably spent more time on Barra in the five years from 1832 to 1837 than he had in the previous twenty-five years put together, but his relations with his kinsmen and tenants were now damaged beyond repair. When he left the island in March 1837 few were sorry to see him go, and he was probably glad to see the last of it. Given the circumstances of his departure and the bad odour which his behaviour had induced, he was fortunate to be able to retreat to his wife's home in Ireland where he could lie low for a while.

The army, and in particular service abroad, offered him an opportunity to recover his financial position, to live in a degree of comfort he would not be able to afford in Britain, and to remove himself from the opprobrium which his behaviour had aroused in some social circles. He joined the 78th Highlanders in full knowledge they were about to sail for India. In India he apparently came unscathed through the fever-induced catastrophe of the Sukhur expedition, but by good fortune or good networking found himself promoted to command a division in the Madras presidency. Madras was a much sought-after posting, being both a pleasant and prosperous place to live but also the most peaceful of the Indian presidencies. When his time was up as divisional commander he was miraculously appointed to the divisional staff in Madras rather than returning to his regiment, thus avoiding service in Aden.

After thirteen years away, he returned to England in a much better financial position than he had left it, and with a regimental colonelcy and the rank of Lieutenant General under his belt. His wife's death within a few days of arriving back in England cast an unexpected shadow over Roderick's return but within three years he had remarried. With Eliza he lived out the last years of his life in some comfort in a spacious town house pampered by half a dozen servants. Although he was never knighted he was elevated to the rank of full General and became Colonel of his old regiment, the 78th Highlanders. So he died both an officer and a gentleman.

But what of the highland chief? There is little reason to think that Roderick ever placed much value on his chiefship of the Clan Macneil. He left Barra when he was sixteen and apart from the last few years of his ownership of the estate he spent little time there. The people of Barra were strangers to him. It is true that in a letter to Angus Macdonald in August 1825 he claims that his approach to the rejuvenation of the estate was initially determined by 'old feudal feelings' but there is nothing in his letters between October 1823 and August 1825 to support this claim. From the first he refers to the people of Barra as tenants, a term his father used in only one of his fourteen preserved letters. He defines his relationship with his clansmen very clearly in the letter which accompanied his 'proclamation' in July 1825: 'if one set of servants (tenants at will are nothing else) won't do, the master must try others'. In the same letter he pours invective on them – they are fickle, idle, stiff-necked, disgraceful, ungrateful. Another letter a week later expands on the theme – they are slothful, negligent, shameful, insubordinate. There are no signs of 'old feudal feelings' here!

Apart from revealing Roderick's indifference to his clansmen, the letters to Angus Macdonald provide useful insights into the General's character. Having correctly identified the key role that Macdonald would play in his relationship with his tenants, he attempted to win the priest's support with a combination of the carrot and the stick: 'I will take care of your interest' but if I don't get your co-operation 'I will bring in Protestant tenants'. In fact he badly misjudged

Macdonald, who made no attempt to act as a genuine intermediary but seems to have actively encouraged both opposition to Macneil's schemes and plans for the 1826 emigration. Although Roderick's father had said of him in 1809 that there was 'a dash of indecision in him', his service in the army seems to have knocked that out of him. His letters to Macdonald are full of clear and precise orders which he expects his tenants to obey. He changed course three times over the way in which the affairs of the estate might be turned around, but on each occasion he embraced the current answer to his problems with enthusiasm and certainty. It is perhaps ironic that a man who his father said 'has no desire for gambling' in the end brought himself and his ancestral estate to ruin by taking a commercial gamble on a colossal scale.

In the prolonged process of sequestration and legal proceedings resulting from his bankruptcy Roderick revealed some of his worst traits. Duplicity, cunning, evasiveness, and downright dishonesty are all to be found in the proceedings in the Sederunt books. Nor was his behaviour much better when he returned to the army, being several times posted as 'absent without leave' as he dragged his heels apparently trying to avoid a posting to South Africa and possibly St Helena. Once in India he may have mended his ways, and certainly he seems to have found friends in the right places, as promotions and staff appointments were given to him. There is even the possibility that he became a popular figure. Captain Ramsay described him as 'a very fine old soldier' and J.A. Ewart said his death was 'to the great regret of everyone connected with the Ross-shire Buffs (78th Highlanders)'.

Twenty years after his death, at the time of the Crofter's Commission, he certainly escaped the opprobrium that was heaped on Gordon of Cluny and Lady Gordon Cathcart (the subsequent landlords of Barra) and Dr M' Gillivray (tenant-farmer at Eoligarry). Some indeed sought to eulogize him. Alexander Carmichael said that 'he was adored by his people', while another contemporary writer described him as 'graceful in person and so beloved by his people'. Did Roderick blush in his grave? Probably not, but he may have been warmed by the occasional visits to his grave which his widow Eliza made for several years after his death, and by the words she had carved on the south side of his mausoleum. Following a brief description of his military service she said: 'He was noble in character, exemplary in every relation of life. A gallant soldier, a warm and generous friend and affectionate husband.'

And he was, beyond question 'The Last Chief of the Ancient Line.'

Sources

Abbreviations used:
BL: British Library
ILN: Illustrated London News
IOR: India Office Records
MQOH: Museum of the Queen's Own Highlanders, Fort George
NAS: National Archives of Scotland
NLS: National Library of Scotland
NSLP: Nova Scotia Land Petitions
PANS: Public Archives of Nova Scotia
PAPEI: Public Archives of Prince Edward Island
PRO: Public Record Office (now the National Archives, London)
RCAHMS: Royal Commissions for Ancient and Historical
    Monuments of Scotland
SCA: Scottish Catholic Archives
SCR: Scots College in Rome
WO: War Office

1. 'From very remote antiquity': The Macneils of Barra

Norse history and archaeology:
A. Anderson, *Early Sources of Scottish History*, (1922(
C. Borgstrom, *The Norse Place-Names of Barra* in J.L. Campbell
    (ed) *The Book of Barra*, (1936)
A. Duncan, *Scotland. The Making of the Kingdom*, (1975)
K. Branigan & P. Foster, *Barra and the Bishop's Isles*, (2002)
J. Graham-Campbell and C. Batey, *Vikings in Scotland – An
    Archaeological Survey*, (1998)

The Macneils:

NAS: GD/201/1/122; 351; GD/202/1/930; GD/201/5/15

Register of the Privy Council X, XI

M. Martin, *A Description of the Western Isles of Scotland*, (1703)

A. Maclean Sinclair, 'The Macneils of Barra', *Celtic Review* 3, (1907)

R.L. Macneil, *The Castle in the Sea*, (1964)

G. Donaldson, *Scotland: James V–VII*, (1978)

J.L. Campbell, 'The Macneils of Barra in the '45', *The Innes Review* 17, (1966)

Kisimul Castle:

RCHAMS: *The Outer Hebrides, Skye and the Smaller Islands*, (1928)

S. Cruden, *The Scottish Castle*, (1960)

D. Pringle, *The Ancient Monuments of the Western Isles*, (1994)

The Clans:

T. Devine, *Clanship to Crofters War*, (1994)

R. Dodgshon, *From Chiefs to Landlords*, (1998)

2. 'A very genteel young man': Colonel Roderick Macneil – Gentleman Farmer

Roderick the Gentle:

NAS: CS/44/446; GD/1/736/13; 54; 93; 170/1585/46; 202/70/8; 202/74/2; 244/34/; TD/85/63(A8)Roll 2

W. Innes Addson (ed), *Matriculation Albums of the University of Glasgow 1728–1858*, (1913)

M. McKay (ed), *The Reverend John Walker's Report on the Hebrides of 1764 and 1771*, (1980)

J.L. Buchanan, *Travels in the Western Hebrides. From 1782 to 1790*, (1793)

E. MacQueen, *The Parish of Barray. The Statistical Account of Scotland 13*, (1794)

E. Burke, *The Mission of St. Patrick, Grand River West*, PAPEI 2353, 245, (1880)

Dept of Agriculture for Scotland, *Eoligarry Estate, Barra*, (R.O.608. E542-50-4/40)

Service in America:

PRO: WO/12/8597

G. Patterson, 'History of Hamiltons Regiment', *Studies in Nova Scotia History*, (1940)

R. Day, *Not a Drum was Heard. The Life of Sir John Moore*, (2001)

Emigration:

K. Branigan, *From Clan to Clearance*, (2005)

J. Bumsted, *The Peoples' Clearance: Highland Emigration to British North America 1770–1815*, (1982)

E. Fraser, *On Emigration from the Scottish Highlands and Islands*, (1802) (unpub manuscript NLS)

J. Lawson, 'Passengers on the *Alexander*', *Island Magazine 29*, (1991)

3. 'As respectable a character as any': Roderick Joins the Army

Roderick's early military career:

NAS: GD/1/76¾5; 46; 91

PRO: WO List 1809, 218; WO 3½248

W. Moorsum, *Historical Record of the 52nd Regiment*, (1860)

H. Davidson, *History and Services of the 78th Highlanders*, (1901)

M. Urban, *Rifles*, (2003)

M. Chappell, *Wellington's Peninsula Regiments:The Light Infantry*, (2004)

The Corunna Campaign:

W. Napier, *History of the War in the Peninsula* Vol.I, (1850)

H. Curling (ed), *The Recollections of Rifleman Harris*, (1848)

C. Hibbert, *Corunna*, (1961)

P. Haythornthwaite, *Corunna 1809*, (2001)

R. Day, *Not a Drum was Heard. The Life of Sir John Moore*, (2001)

4. 'His bones are healed': Battle Fever & Promotion

Return from Corunna:
NAS: GD/1/736/93; 101; GD/453/16
PRO: WO List 1811, 318
J.L. Campbell (ed), *The Book of Barra* (The Macneil Letters, 20 April 1809), (1936)
Walcheren and Bergen-op-Zoom:
PRO: WO31/304; WO List 1815, 296
E. Hathway (ed), *A True Soldier Gentleman*, (2000)
H. Curling (ed), *The Recollections of Rifleman Harris*, (1848)
R.D. Henegan, *Seven Years Campaigning in the Peninsula and the Netherlands*, (1846)
R. Dunn-Pattison, *The History of the 91st Argyllshire Highlanders*, (1910)
G. Bond, *The Grand Expedition: The British Invasion of Holland in 1809*, (1999)
W. Leeson, *British Minor Expeditions Pt.III*, (1985)
A. Bamford, *The British Army in the Low Countries 1813–14*
J. van Gorkum, *De Bestorming der vesting Bergen op Zoom 8 Sten Maart 1814*, (1862)

5. 'There is a prospect of more': A Battle, a Wedding & a Death

Quatre Bras and Waterloo:
PRO: WO List 1816, 177; WO List 1817, 181; WO 3¼12.
H.T. Siborne, *Waterloo Letters*, (1891)
B. Foster, *Wellington's Light Cavalry*, (1982)
I.Fletcher, *Wellington's Regiments*, (1994)
P. Haythornthwaite, *Wellington's Military Machine*, (1989)
D. Hamilton Williams, *Waterloo. New Perspectives*, (1993)
C. Dalton, *The Waterloo Roll Call with Biographical Notes and Anecdotes (2nd Ed)*, (1904)
Roderick the Gentle:
NAS: GD/1/736/91, 94.

J.L. Campbell (ed), *The Book of Barra* (The Macneil Letters from 6 June 1816 to 9 August 1821), (1936)

J. Macculloch, *A Description of the Western Islands of Scotland* Vols.I and III, (1819)

Gores Liverpool Street Directory, 1810, 1814

Gores Liverpool Trade Directory, 1821, 1823

R. Griffiths, *The History of the Royal and Ancient Park of Toxteth, Liverpool*, (1907)

Liverpool Mercury: 26 April 1822

Emigration 1817 and 1821:

PANS: RG.1/Vol.239/Doc.109; RG5, GP.Vol.7; RG11/1, 178–9; NSLP 1818

PRO: CO217/53; 135; CO/384/2; T11/58; T29/148

D. Dobson, *Ships from Scotland to America 1628–1828* Vol.I, (1998)

K. Branigan, *From Clan to Clearance*, (2005)

The Life Guards:

PRO: WO List 1818, 511; 1819, 511; 1820, 115; 1822, 258; 1823, 118

PRO: HO44/9

H. Arbuthnot, *The Journal of Mrs Arbuthnot*, (1950)

6. 'I was literally tied to the stake': Roderick Becomes Chief

The Estate in Trust:

NAS: RD/5/223, 364–95; TD 85/63/A8; GD 202/37; 244/35/bundle 2

NAS: CS 44/Box 446.

Roderick's Strategy:

J.L. Campbell (ed), *The Book of Barra* (27 October 1823 – 18 October 1825) (1936)

NAS: GD/46/17/Vol.70; CS 96/4274

SRO: D593K, 1/3/28

Emigration 1825–6:

SCR: Box 12/109; 127

SCA: BL5/170; 192
PANS: Vol 335, Doc.64
K. Branigan, *From Clan to Clearance*, (163–4), (2005)

7. 'A large and expensive works': The Industrial Revolution Comes to Barra

Kelp Production and the Chemical Factory:
J. Bumstead, 'The Rise and Fall of the Kelping Industry in the Western
    Isles' in K. Branigan *From Clan to Clearance*, 123–38, (2005)
SCR: B12/132; 136; 138
SCA: BL6/134
NAS: GD201/Pt5/1232/8–9; GD244/35; CS96/4274, 39–41
Inverness Courier, 19 February 1850, 4
R. Stevenson, *Report on Northern Lighthouses to the Commissioners
    of Northern Lights* (NLS: Acc 10706, 92–4, 1834, 1837, 1838
K. Branigan, *From Clan to Clearance* 34–6, (2005)
Debts and Loans:
NAS: CS96/4274; GD 244/35
Liverpool Mercury, 11 March 1889
Liverpool Courier, 15 March 1889
Rents and Tenants:
SCR: B12/128; 129; 136; 138
NAS: CS96/4274, 25; CS44/B446
Capt Henderson and the *Fleece*:
The Belfast News-Letter, Issue 10087, 14 February 1834

8. 'His Majesty's rebel': Roderick Goes Bankrupt

The principal sources for this chapter are the three Sederunt books
    NAS: CS 96/4274, 4275, 4276.
Horning:
NAS: GD 244/35

Debts:

NAS: *General Register of Inhibitions and Interdictions*, Vol. 397, 24 August 1836; 19 November 1836

NAS: GD 244/34, Bundle 1

Eoligarry and the Sale of the Estate:

NAS: CS96/4274, 154–55; 4275, 25–30, 37, 49

K. Branigan, *From Clan to Clearance*, 146–8, (2005)

9. 'This is a very unwholesome country': Roderick Takes the Queen's Rupee

Army promotions:

WO List: 1838, 481; 1843, 274

WO: 12/8341–45; 12/9273–75; 31/755, 841

Regimental News, (1st Battn Argyll & Sutherland Highlanders) Pitermaritzburg, No.16, May 1855, 3

Service in India, Poona:

MQOH: L17(565)

WO List: 1847; WO 31/912

Bombay Almanac, 1843–1846

ILN: 6 April 1844; 7 December 1844

Army List, 11848–49, 340

R. Parsons, *Migrant Ships for South Australia 1836–1860*

T. Heathcote, *The Indian Army*, (1976)

B.D.W. Ramsey, *Rough Recollections of Military Service and Society*, (1885)

Service in India, Madras:

WO List: 1855/56

BL: IOR L/AG/23/10; L/MIL/15/84; *East India Register*, 1851–54

Madras Almanac: 1852

ILN: 26 April 1851

F. Boase, *Modern English Biography* (1882) Vol.I, 96, (1897)

W.J. Wilson, *History of the Madras Army*, (1882)

H. Hart, *The New Army and Militia List for 1855*, (1855)

10. 'The gallant General': Roderick's Return

Return to England:
Madras Almanac: 1856, (for 1854–5)
D. Howarth and S. Howarth, *The P&O Story*, (1986)
Southampton Register of Births and Deaths: 1855, 165
New Calcutta Directory: 1856, 1858, 1859
London Gazette: 1855, pt 2, no.21690; 6 April 1855
L.C. Jackson, *History of the United Services Club*
Second Marriage:
Hanover Square Register: 13 January 1844
BL: East India Register: 1825, 1826, 1830, 1831
Hampshire Advertiser: 13 January 1844
Prerogative Court of Canterbury Prob. 6/208, 1d, 26, 255
1861 Census of Great Britain
PRO: Probate 1½206
Final Military Appointments:
London Gazette: 1860, Issue 22395, May–June
London Gazette: 1863 May/June; Issue 22701, January–February
Gentleman's Magazine: December 1863, 806–7

11. 'He was noble in character': Roderick in Retrospect

NAS: GD/1/736/93
J.A. Ewart, *The Story of a Soldier's Life*, 305, (1881)
Quarterly Review: 1895, 117
A. Carmichael, *Grazing and Agrestic Customs of the Outer Hebrides*,
    Report of the Crofter's Commission Appendix A, (1883)
Southampton Cemetery Committee Minutes: 23 November 1867;
    21 March 1868

Acknowledgements

I have been helped in many ways by many people in researching and writing this book and I am pleased to have the opportunity to say a heartfelt 'thank you' to them all.

I am grateful to the staff of the following archives for their help and advice in searching their collections:

The British Library
National Records Office, Kew
National Archives of Scotland
Edinburgh City Library
Scottish Catholic Archives
Staffordshire Records Office
The National Army Museum
Oxford & Bucks Light Infantry Museum
The Greenjackets Museum
The Queen's Own Highlanders Regimental Museum
The King's Regiment Museum
The Scots College at Rome
Halifax Citadel, Parks Canada

I am especially grateful to those individuals who have helped to access information in these and other archives:

Lottie Boutell
Lawrie Butler
Dr Martin Dearne
Col. Angus Fairrie
Dr Christine Johnson
Dino Lemonofides
Christa Mee

Wayne Moug (Halifax, Canada)
Geoff Watts
Helen Whyte (Ottawa, Canada)
The late John Macinnes

For encouragement and help in researching the wider history of Barra I am very grateful to Ian and Nancy Macneil of Barra, to Calum and Rhoda Macneil, to Chrissie and the late Niall Macpherson, to David and Diana Savory, John Allan Macneil, and Angie Foster. I am also indebted to my colleagues Patrick Foster, David Gilbertson and Colin Merrony for their support over the many years of fieldwork on Barra. I am grateful for information supplied by Ben Buxton and Robert Lindzee Gordon.

For help and advice in preparing the book for publication I must thank Dr Jim Symonds and Anna Badcock. Publication would not have been possible also without the generosity of the Robert Kiln Trust. Indeed, but for their initial support in 1988, there would have been no SEARCH project and hence no research into the archaeology and history of Barra and ultimately of the General.

In collecting illustrations together I must acknowledge the generous help of Ian Fletcher and Philip Haythornthwaite in illustrating aspects of the General's military career. Other illustrations have been tracked down and/or provided by Ian Harte, Christa Mee, David Savory, Jim Symonds, and Geoff Watts. I am also pleased to acknowledge the permissions for illustrations to be used provided by The British Library, The National Archives of Scotland, the P&O Co., the RCHAMS, and the State Library of Victoria, Australia.

The photographs of the portraits of Colonel Roderick Macneil of Barra and Jean Cameron Macneil of Barra were provided by Ian Roderick Macneil of Barra (©), from photographic copies of the portraits given to him by the late Henry S. MacNeil. The original portraits remain in a private collection the owners of which hold the copyright on them. Macneil of Barra wishes to express his appreciation to Henry S. MacNeil for his gift and to his daughter, Mrs Barbara McNeil Jordan, for permission to reproduce the photographs in this book. Further reproduction is prohibited.

Needless to say, the author is particularly grateful to Ian Macneil of Barra for his help in acquiring copies of Raeburn's portraits of Roderick the Gentle and Jean Cameron, and to Mrs Barbara McNeil Jordan for permission to use these in the book.

Most of all I am grateful to Nong who not only offered her usual encouragement and help, but also remained remarkably cheerful throughout the experience of living with two grumpy old men rather than just one.

List of Illustrations

—

41. The *Bussorah Merchant* (courtesy of the La Trobe Collection, State Library of Victoria)
42. A nineteenth-century view of Poona (H. Salt, courtesy of the British Library)
43. A European house at Madras (J. Gantz, courtesy of the British Library)
44. Government House at Madras. (H. Merke, 1807)
45. The P&O steamship *Hindostan* (© P&O Heritage Collection, DP World)
46. The port of Suez in the mid-nineteenth century (L'Illustration, 1863)
47. A way station on the overland route from Suez to the Nile (© P&O Heritage Collection, DP World)
48. The Dolphin Hotel, Southampton (photo: Geoff Watts)
49. The coat of arms on Macneil's mausoleum (photo: Geoff Watts)
50. The United Services Club in Pall Mall (1858, artist unknown)
51. St George's Church, Hanover Square, London (photo: the author)
52. Hyde Park Gardens, where Roderick died in 1863 (photo: the author)
53. General Macneil as Colonel of the 78th Highlanders (artist unknown, photographic copy courtesy of the Museum of the Queen's Own Highlanders)
54. Roderick and Isabella's mausoleum, Southampton (photo: Geoff Watts)

Index

Also available from Amberley Publishing

'Remarkably vivid... reads like a horror thriller' THE SCOTS MAGAZINE

JOHN SADLER

Glencoe
The Infamous Massacre 1692

The story of the Campbell massacre of the
MacDonald Clan, one of the most emotive
episodes in Scottish history

A startling new history of the Campbell massacre of the McDonald Clan, one of the most emotive episodes in Scottish history

'Handsomely produced and lavishly illustrated... a very readable book' HISTORY SCOTLAND

'Much new information has been unearthed — all marshalled here with admirable clarity and skill' THE SCOTSMAN

'Remarkably vivid... reads like a horror thriller' THE SCOTS MAGAZINE

£12.99 Paperback
32 illustrations (25 colour)
304 pages
978-1-84868-515-4

Available from all good bookshops or to order direct
Please call **01285-760-030**
www.amberley-books.com